Career Coaching for Midlife and Beyond

A Practical Handbook

Denise Taylor

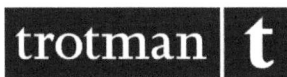

Career Coaching for Midlife and Beyond

This first edition published in 2025 by Trotman, an imprint of Trotman Indigo Publishing Ltd, 18e Charles Street, Bath BA1 1HX.

© Trotman Indigo Publishing Ltd 2025

Author: Dr Denise Taylor

British Library Cataloguing in Publication Data
A catalogue record for this book is available from the British Library.

Paperback ISBN 978-1-911724-71-1
eISBN 978-1-911724-72-8

All rights reserved. This book is sold subject to the condition that it shall not, by way of trade or otherwise, be lent, resold, hired out or otherwise circulated without the publisher's prior written consent in any form of binding or cover other than that in which it is published and without a similar condition including this condition being imposed on the subsequent purchaser. No part of this publication may be reproduced, stored in a retrieval system or transmitted in any form or by any means, electronic and mechanical, photocopying, recording or otherwise without prior permission of Trotman Indigo Publishing.

Every effort has been made to trace copyright holders and to obtain their permission for the use of copyright material. The publisher apologises for any errors or omissions, and would be grateful to be notified of any corrections that should be incorporated in future editions of this book.

The authorised representative in the EEA is Easy Access System Europe Oü (EAS), Mustamäe tee 50, 10621 Tallinn, Estonia.

Printed and bound in the UK by CMP Ltd.

 All details in this book were correct at the time of going to press. To keep up to date with all the latest news and updates and to access the online resources that accompany this book, use this QR code or visit **www.trotman.co.uk/pages/career-coaching-for-midlife-and-beyond-resources**

Contents

About the author	vii
Acknowledgements	ix
Foreword	xi
Introduction: Why stories matter	xiii
How to use this book	xv
List of 40 coaching tools	xvii

Chapter 1 Why midlife and retirement coaching matters — 1
- Setting the context: The diversity of the 50+ client group — 1
- The demographic and social shifts — 2
- Redefining work and retirement — 5
- Psychological transitions in later life — 7
- Why career coaching must evolve — 9
- What this book offers — 10

Chapter 2 Understanding midlife career transitions — 13
- Introduction — 13
- The landscape of midlife career change — 14
- The emotional and psychological journey — 16
- Confidence, locus of control, and mindset — 19
- Cultural and contextual influences — 24
- Retirement on the horizon — 26
- Health, energy, and unexpected life events — 27
- Redefining success in midlife — 29
- The coach's role — 31
- Positive affirmations and visualisation — 32
- Closing reflections — 33

Chapter 3 Coaching for career reinvention in midlife — 35
- The nature of career reinvention — 35
- Strategic positioning and personal branding — 38
- Translating skills and experience — 43
- Networking with purpose — 48
- Digital presence and visibility — 52
- Positioning for flexible work and phased retirement — 55
- When life affects work: Health, caregiving, and relationships — 59
- The coach's role in reinvention — 62
- Closing reflections — 63

Chapter 4 The psychology of retirement and identity shifts   65
Retirement as an identity transition   65
Understanding the retirement transition   66
When retirement isn't a choice   67
Beyond paid work: The value of unpaid contribution   68
Identity, purpose, and the changing self   68
Life stage coaching   74
Generativity and giving back   75
Identity beyond job titles   77
The psychology of transition: Seven key factors   80
The role of relationships   81
Navigating internalised ageism   86
Resilience and health planning   87
Purpose in later life   89
Rebuilding rhythm: Structure and routine   92
Closing reflections   92

Chapter 5 Designing a meaningful life after full-time work   95
The shift from career to life design   95
Rediscovering purpose and value   96
Time, rhythm, and the reshaping of days   98
Social connection and the quiet drift   99
Contribution and the value of unpaid work   101
Creativity, curiosity, and new joys   104
When life shifts unexpectedly   105
Life as prototype: Small experiments, big shifts   107
A word on joy   108
Closing reflections   109

Chapter 6 Practical tools for career coaches   113
The role of tools in midlife and later-life career coaching   113
Foundations of effective coaching tools   114
(St)Age-specific coaching approaches   115
Core coaching tools and exercises   118
Working with complexity   136
Integrating tools into the coaching journey   137
Adapting coaching questions for midlife and later-life clients   140
Closing reflections   141

Chapter 7 Case studies: Navigating complex career transitions — 145
Introduction — 145
Transitions triggered by work and life disruption — 146
Transitions shaped by life events — 153
Identity-led transitions — 156
What these stories reveal about later-life coaching — 157

Chapter 8 Navigating ageism and changing workplace dynamics — 159
A subtle and persistent bias — 159
Understanding ageism in context — 160
Reframing identity and value — 164
Claiming adaptability and curiosity — 165
Adapting to the new world of work — 168
Working across generations — 169
Accommodations and health-supportive strategies — 172
Rethinking employability in later life — 174
Finding the right workplace fit — 176
Closing reflections — 178

Chapter 9 Portfolio careers, self-employment, encore careers, and unretirement — 181
Redefining work in later life — 181
Portfolio careers: Designing a richer tapestry of work and life — 182
Stepping into self-employment: Freedom with purpose — 187
Encore careers: Purpose-driven work in later life — 191
Unretirement: Returning with intention — 193
Navigating the emotional terrain of reinvention — 197
Practical tools and pathways — 199
Closing reflections: Crafting work that fits — 203

Chapter 10 Coaching with integrity: Ethical and psychological grounding in later life — 205
Holding space with integrity and care — 205
The psychological landscape of later-life clients — 206
Ethical boundaries and responsibilities — 209
Reflective practice and supervision in later-life career coaching — 212
Final reflections: The ethical invitation — 215

Chapter 11 Coaching at the edge of change: Supporting what comes after work — 217

- Looking back — 217
- Future landscape — 218
- Evolving role of the coach — 219
- Technology and AI — 220
- Life review and meaning — 221
- Developing the coach's reflective practice — 221
- Closing reflections — 222

Looking ahead: Deeper reflections on life after work — 225

Further reading and sources by chapter — 227

About the author

Dr Denise Taylor is a Chartered Psychologist and award-winning Career and Retirement Coach who has spent over 40 years helping people navigate changing work landscapes and major life transitions. With a doctorate earned at 64 focused on meaningful ageing, she brings both academic depth and personal experience to her work.

Denise has written eight books on careers, midlife transitions, and later life, and has delivered pre-retirement seminars since the 1980s. Her work challenges outdated notions of retirement, offering instead a reimagined view of later life as a time of purpose, possibility, and personal growth.

Now in her late 60s, Denise combines professional coaching and thought leadership with a deep connection to nature, tending her own woodland in rural Gloucestershire and leading retreats that support reflection and renewal. Whether through writing, coaching, or public speaking, she invites others to step into later life with confidence, curiosity, and intention.

Find out more at:

 denisetaylor.co.uk/book
 linkedin.com/in/denisetaylor
 ageingreimagined.substack.com
 youtube.com/@BeyondMidlifeDeniseTaylor

Acknowledgements

This book was shaped not only at my desk but also among the trees.

To the wood that held me through endings and beginnings, your quiet rhythms, fierce stillness, and seasons of renewal made this possible.

Thank you for reminding me how to listen.

My deep thanks to Sarah Taylor Phillips of Career Voyage for her generous encouragement, thoughtful questions, and careful reading of the draft. Her support helped clarify the shape of this work.

I am also grateful to Oliver Jenkin and Alexandra Price, for their careful editorial guidance, and to the team at Trotman, for their support in bringing this book to publication.

Finally, to the many clients and colleagues who shared their experiences with honesty and courage: your stories are woven throughout these pages. This book would not exist without you.

And to the trees, still standing, still teaching – I carry your wisdom forward, a reminder that renewal is always possible and that listening, deeply, is where new beginnings take root.

Foreword

Ageing and the latter stages of our lives can sometimes seem like the 'elephant in the room' in career development discourse. Granted, books and articles have been written to help support individuals over 50, but at a time when individuals are choosing (for a variety of reasons, some self-driven, others less so) to continue working or re-enter work in their sixties or beyond, age is a theme that will only become more important for individuals working with adults in the latter years of their lives. This is a theme that is starting to feel close to home for me – as I write this, I am four months away from my forty-ninth birthday and I am no different from many people in my sense of being older, with everything that this implies for my sense of identity and of where I am in my career.

The book you hold, written by a writer with immense experience in the field of career coaching for older adults, fills an important gap in the career development literature. Dr Denise Taylor writes with immense wisdom and sensitivity, framing what it means to support individuals in mid-life and beyond holistically, underlining the varied psychological shifts that can occur for individuals in their 50s, 60s and 70s. Addressing ageist myths about what older individuals are capable of, Dr Taylor nonetheless does not sugar coat what it means to be an individual seeking work at a time of life when many planned to enter retirement. Each individual's circumstances vary, but the reader is ably supported by chapters looking at a range of situations, from those seeking to re-enter work when retirement is less fulfilling than they anticipated, to those having to find work through financial necessity.

Those who are considering reorientating their practice to work with older clients will find much useful information in this book to help with this, including a wide range of practical activities designed for different types of client and different stages of the coaching process. Throughout, Dr Taylor maintains an ethically grounded focus, helping the reader maintain a reflective awareness of what areas fall within their remit as a coach, and which needs would be more appropriately met by a different type of professional.

A vital book, whose importance will only grow as longer, less linear careers become more and more the norm. I wholeheartedly recommend it to all who have a genuine interest in supporting adults throughout the length of their career journey.

Dr Oliver Jenkin PGCE RCDP, NICEC Fellow.
CDI Senior Professional Development and Standards Manager, and Editor of the CDI's magazine, Career Matters.
August 2025

Introduction: Why stories matter

This book is filled with stories, real, textured, human stories, because that's how we learn best. Not from lists or lectures, but from lived experience. During a Wilderness Guides retreat, we sat around the fire and spoke about the power of story, and we listened to stories. Stories bring aliveness. They carry emotion, meaning, and memory. They don't just inform us; they stay with us, shaping how we see ourselves and others.

In my work as a later-life career coach and wilderness rites of passage guide, I've seen time and again how stories create connection. They open the door to reflection, understanding, and possibility. The case studies in this book are more than examples; they are windows into the complex realities of midlife and later-life transitions. Each one holds a thread of truth that may resonate with your clients, colleagues, or perhaps even yourself.

I wrote this book to offer something real and grounded. Not a blueprint or a fix, but a companion for coaches supporting people navigating change in the second half of life. I bring to it my decades of experience, my research, and my deep belief in the capacity of people to reinvent, to contribute, and to grow at any age.

As you read, take time to consider the people you've worked with and those you know. How do these stories relate to them? What echoes do you hear? Start to capture your own, because the stories you carry, and the ones you help others to tell, are part of the larger conversation about what it means to live and work meaningfully in later life.

How to use this book

This book is designed as both a reflective companion and a practical resource for career professionals working with midlife and later-life clients. Whether you are a qualified coach, psychologist, or midlife specialist, you'll find tools, case studies, and insights to deepen your practice and support clients through meaningful career transitions.

Midlife and retirement coaching is inherently holistic. It draws on career development theory, adult life-stage psychology, narrative practice, and life design. By 'life design', I just mean creating a fulfilling life in the round, not any one formal model. It's about more than job search; it's about identity, purpose, renewal, and navigating change with insight and intention.

It can be read cover to cover or dipped into as needed, by theme, client scenario, or tool.

Types of tools you'll find

To make navigation easier, tools are grouped into the following formats:

- **Practical tools**
  A wide range of activities to use directly with your clients. Some will be found as downloadable handouts from https://denisetaylor.co.uk/book/
- **Coaching prompts**
  Questions to use directly in sessions – for exploration, insight, or forward movement.
- **Reflective practice**
  Widely used in coach training contexts, this is about you as the coach thinking about your own process, not guiding a client through something.

How to engage with this book

Read the case studies as inspiration, not templates.
Each vignette is grounded in real coaching experience and shows the emotional nuance behind career decisions in later life.

Use the tools flexibly.
You don't need to follow every prompt or activity. Choose what feels most relevant to your client's context, readiness, and energy.

Pause for your own reflection.
Many prompts are equally useful for the coach. Notice what resonates in you as you support others through change.

Revisit chapters as your practice evolves.
This book is designed to grow with you, offering insight not just into your clients' journeys, but your own.

List of 40 coaching tools

2.1	Confidence tracker	22
2.2	Control wheel	22
2.3	Three coaching questions to reframe retirement	27
3.1	From title to value	39
3.2	Skills mapping: Seeing transferable strengths	46
3.3	Designing your ideal week	58
4.1	Rituals for closure	72
4.2	Legacy reflection exercise: What do you want to leave behind?	76
4.3	The relationship wheel: Mapping connection and belonging	84
4.4	Plan B mapping	88
4.5	Finding purpose	91
4.6	Time mapping exercise	92
5.1	Time mapping for meaning	98
5.2	Social circle mapping	100
5.3	Contribution inventory	102
6.1	Life timeline exercise	119
6.2	Translating skills and experience worksheet	120
6.3	Values and priorities clarifier	121
6.4	Retirement mindset assessment	122
6.5	Roles and identity mapping	123
6.6	Energy and time use audit	124
6.7	Work–life grid	125
6.8	Designing a week	126
6.9	Purpose and contribution cards	127
6.10	Health and capacity reflection tool	128
6.11	Creative expression prompts	129
6.12	Joy mapping	130
6.13	Legacy interview or audio memoir prompt	131
6.14	The interesting inventory	132
6.15	Emotional validation activity	133
6.16	Role-based identity mapping	133
6.17	Gentle narrative work	134
6.18	Life review techniques	134
6.19	Legacy projects	135
6.20	Identity anchors	135
6.21	Curiosity-led exploration	136
9.1	Is self-employment right for me?	190
9.2	Rethinking retirement, what's next for me?	196
9.3	Who am I becoming now?	198
9.4	Exploratory exercise: Designing a portfolio map or weekly rhythm	200
9.5	Moving from ideas to action	202

Chapter 1
Why midlife and retirement coaching matters

> **Summary**
>
> *As people live and work longer, career transitions in midlife and beyond are becoming more complex and more personal. This chapter explores why coaching at this stage requires more than tools and tactics. It calls for presence, psychological depth, and space to explore identity, purpose, and possibility in later life. We'll draw on both theory and real-life stories to show why it matters.*

Setting the context: The diversity of the 50+ client group

Clients aged 50 and above are far from a homogeneous group. They range from people in their early 50s through to people in their 70s and 80s, each with distinct needs, motivations, and life circumstances. Some urgently need income and are actively job seeking. Others, financially secure, work for stimulation, structure, identity, or social connection. They may have children at home, support elderly parents, or juggle both responsibilities. For some, work offers identity and purpose; for others, it provides social connection or mental stimulation. Others continue working out of financial necessity. Coaches must listen carefully to understand each client's unique resources, challenges, and aspirations.

Consider Amy, in her late 50s, who has spent decades building her professional identity. Now, she feels uncertain – not ready to retire but not eager to continue as before. She wonders what's next. Amy's experience is increasingly common. Many midlife and beyond clients seek fulfilment, autonomy, or something new, rather than traditional career progression or retirement. This is where midlife and retirement coaching becomes crucial.

While Amy is seeking a slower, more reflective shift, others are keen to reengage at full speed.

This book starts with the premise that coaching individuals aged 50 and above isn't a niche; it's increasingly central. As people live longer, healthier lives, boundaries between work and retirement blur, making coaching essential for navigating transitions with purpose and clarity.

Consider Sarah, who previously ran a multimillion-pound business and stepped back to raise a family. Now, at 60, with children not yet at university, she's eager to restart her career, and slowing down isn't part of her vocabulary.

Contrast this with Julian, who was made redundant from his role as a marketing director and seeks professional advice due to concerns that his age is affecting his job search. His retirement finances were built around another decade of work.

Julian's experience resonates with many midlife professionals facing age discrimination and employment uncertainty.

James, a garage supervisor, faces retirement pressure from his employer but worries about losing social structure and becoming isolated. He's uncertain about his future direction.

Then there's Amira, who hasn't worked since her children were born. After her husband's sudden death revealed financial insecurity, she now urgently needs employment but feels inadequate and overwhelmed by this shift.

These diverse stories illustrate the complexity of midlife career coaching. Each client brings unique experiences, necessitating a flexible, individualised approach.

The demographic and social shifts

Living longer, working longer

We are living and working longer. In many countries, life expectancy has increased significantly over recent decades, and with it, the age of retirement has steadily moved upwards.

I remember my first job, aged 16 in 1973. My boss was retiring on his 60th birthday. He was given a set of golf clubs as a leaving present. He had never played golf, but wasn't that what you did in retirement? As I looked out the window, I saw him walk away, looking sad and old. But he was only 60.

Back then, retirement was often a sharp transition from work to leisure. At one point, when company pension funds were still buoyant, people were even encouraged to leave in their early 50s, not to find another job, but to begin a life of rest and recreation, freeing up work for younger employees. That model now feels out of sync with how we live today.

We now understand that we need to be active, to have purpose, to feel challenged. These elements keep us younger, healthier, and more fulfilled. Remaining engaged, whether through paid work, volunteering, or creative pursuits, supports our cognitive and emotional wellbeing. Extended working lives are not only more common but often beneficial.

Traditional retirement at 60 or 65 is no longer a universal endpoint. From April 2026, the state pension age will increase to 67 (*UK Government, DWP, 2024*), and current demographic and economic trends suggest it may rise further, possibly to 70. The concept of a fixed retirement age is fading.

Many people continue working into their 70s, sometimes out of necessity, but increasingly out of choice. Through my research and coaching experience, I've found that many stay in their jobs partly from inertia. It can feel easier to keep going than to step back and decide what's next. Making big life decisions or going through the process of applying for something new can feel daunting, especially when the next step isn't yet clear.

This is where career professionals can play a vital role. Rather than defaulting to the status quo, we can help clients explore what they want from their future. We can encourage reflection, broaden their sense of possibility, and offer tools to help them take thoughtful, informed steps forward.

I often refer to the ages of 60–75 (maybe 80) as a golden window: a time when health and energy are usually still intact, and people have a rare combination of freedom and capacity. It's a phase when reinvention is still possible, meaningful contribution is deeply rewarding, and experimentation can lead to surprising fulfilment.

Yet too many people arrive at their mid-70s with regrets, wishing they had taken a leap, tried something new, or lived differently while they still had the chance. Helping clients envisage that possibility earlier can be one of the most powerful interventions we offer.

> **We're all getting older: Time to reframe what that means**
>
> By 2030, more than half of UK adults will be aged 50 or over. And by 2031, the youngest Millennials will reach 50 too. This isn't just about ageing populations; it's about recognising that ageing is no longer a marginal experience. It is the new normal. Yet many people in their 50s and 60s still feel older than everyone else. Some carry internalised images of what 50 or 60 used to mean, even as today's reality looks very different.
>
> The idea of a 'demographic tsunami' can sound ominous, but it can also be a wake-up call, an invitation to reframe ageing as an active, creative, and extended phase of life. Not something to fear, but something to prepare for and shape with intention.

Challenging the four-stage life model

The traditional four-stage model of life: education, work, retirement, and old age, no longer reflects the realities of today's world. Life stages have become more fluid. A 62-year-old might enrol in university. A 68-year-old might launch a consultancy. Someone in their late 50s might scale back their hours to start a creative venture on the side. And, me, at 63 shifted to more nature based work. The once-clear boundaries that defined life phases are blurring.

For career professionals, this means we must move beyond linear models. Supporting clients over 50 requires an openness to hybrid lives, evolving identities, and new beginnings. It means helping people imagine possibilities that don't fit traditional paths and providing support as they navigate transitions that can be exciting, complex, or both.

This shift isn't just about numbers. It reflects broader changes in how society views ageing, productivity, and value. The older workforce is more diverse than ever, encompassing high-flyers, part-time workers, self-employed professionals, career changers, and those seeking a phased transition towards retirement. Midlife and later life can bring a unique kind of wisdom. Clients often draw on a wealth of lived experience, lessons learned from what worked and what didn't.

Yet not everyone adapts readily. Some people resist change, hold on to outdated beliefs, or feel left behind in a fast-moving world. A small minority rest on past experience, haven't kept up to date, and aren't interested in learning new things. Part of our role as coaches is to challenge these limiting mindsets with care and curiosity.

Later life also brings complex realities. Some clients are caring for ageing parents or supporting grandchildren. Others may still have children at home or at university, even as they approach state pension age. Health issues, financial insecurity, or age discrimination can be very real barriers. And while some clients feel liberated by this stage of life, others may feel stuck, invisible, or uncertain.

We cannot approach this group as a monolith. Unlike younger cohorts, such as recent graduates or early career professionals, older clients differ dramatically in life experience, financial circumstances, and emotional needs. One might be starting over after redundancy; another reinventing themselves post-divorce; another navigating work while managing chronic illness. It's why I often say: *'when you've met one 60-year-old, you've met one 60-year-old'*.

To coach effectively in later life, we need to understand the full picture: longer lives, changing social norms, shifting economic conditions, and the emotional complexity of ageing. It calls for empathy, curiosity, and flexibility, alongside the practical tools to support decision-making and reinvention.

Redefining work and retirement

Retirement as a social construct in flux

What we think of as retirement has changed radically over the past hundred years. When state pension schemes were introduced in the 1930s, they were designed for a population with far shorter life expectancies. In many cases, people didn't live long enough to collect their pension. Retirement wasn't so much a life stage as a brief period of rest, if it happened at all.

By the 1970s and 1980s, with rising life expectancy and the expansion of generous company pension schemes, retirement took on a new meaning. It became associated with leisure, reward, and escape, the so-called 'golden years'. For some, it was a time of travel, hobbies, or rest after decades of hard work.

But those assumptions no longer hold. Today, fewer people have access to secure or generous pensions. We are living much longer, often into our 90s, which means retirement can last 20 or 30 years and more. This extended post-work phase demands a fundamental rethink.

Retirement is no longer a single event or a cliff-edge departure from work. Instead, it has become a series of transitions, shaped by personal choice, health, finances, and social context. Some ease out of work gradually; others take breaks and return; many blend paid work, volunteering, caregiving, or creative projects well into their 70s.

Rather than withdrawing from life, many now view retirement as a chance to refocus, reimagine, and renew. It's a time to rethink identity, purpose, and how to use time meaningfully. As a social construct, retirement is still evolving, and we, as career professionals, need to evolve with it.

Beyond the numbers: Expanding the definition of retirement readiness

Retirement is often still defined by financial metrics: pension forecasts, investment returns, and cost-of-living projections. Yet many people arrive at retirement technically 'ready' and emotionally unprepared. Behind the façade of leisure and freedom, some experience a loss of identity, purpose, or social connection.

Clients sometimes express this in stark terms; one individual shared, *'Once I stopped working, I felt like I didn't matter to anyone anymore.'* This sense of invisibility or emotional displacement is not uncommon and can be overlooked by even the most well-meaning advisers or support networks.

A more holistic approach to retirement readiness recognises the importance of emotional, psychological, and relational wellbeing. As coaches, we play a key role in helping individuals prepare not just to retire *from* work, but to retire *into* a life that feels purposeful and connected.

Introducing the concept of the 'Y-olds'

I use the term 'Y-olds', short for 'young-olds', to describe those aged roughly 60 to 75 or 80 who are between full-time work and old age. It's a phrase that emerged during my research and writing, and it captures a distinct and growing group of individuals. These are people who are no longer primarily defined by career or parenting roles, yet who don't identify with the label of 'old age' either.

Y-olds are physically active, intellectually curious, and deeply motivated to live meaningfully. They want to work on their own terms, contribute in ways that matter, and explore new dimensions of life. They're not simply seeking leisure or rest; they're pursuing vitality, relevance, joy, and purposeful engagement. As coaches, recognising and working with this energetic and engaged group means we must challenge outdated stereotypes about ageing and offer frameworks that reflect their lived reality.

The meaning of work naturally evolves over the life course. In early adulthood, work often centres on building identity, achieving success, and securing financial stability. But in midlife and beyond, different questions begin to surface:

How do I want to spend my time? What matters most now? What do I want my legacy to be?

Yet it's important not to generalise. For some clients, midlife still involves ambitious career goals: promotions, scaling businesses, or building a professional legacy. Personally, during my 50s and early 60s, I remained highly career-focused, running a thriving private practice. But the impact of COVID-19, alongside my doctoral research, marked a turning point. I shifted pace and priorities, purchasing four acres of woodland, and I'm finding new meaning in nature, woodland management, and running retreats. I would never have imagined this path just a few years earlier.

That's the reality of later life today: it's fluid, surprising, and deeply personal. Retirement is no longer a single moment of departure from work; it can be a period of reinvention, experimentation, creativity, or contribution. For some, it's about launching a business or pursuing a long-held passion. For others, it's about slowing down or giving back through mentoring and volunteering. And for many, it's about navigating uncertainty: trying to define what later life even means for them.

Traditional assumptions no longer hold. Leisure isn't always fulfilling. Full-time work isn't always sustainable. The path forward is rarely linear.

This is why coaching matters so profoundly at this life stage. It offers a safe, reflective space to explore transitions, both internal and external. It enables clients to surface what truly matters, test new directions, and build clarity about how they want to live and work in this next phase of life.

Psychological transitions in later life

Midlife and beyond are marked by significant psychological transitions, prompting re-evaluation of identity, purpose, and priorities. Developmental theorists such as Jung and Erikson provide valuable frameworks for understanding these changes.

Carl Jung and the inner journey
Carl Jung emphasised the importance of midlife as the start of a critical psychological shift. While psychology had typically focused on childhood, Jung recognised midlife as equally important. Early adulthood focuses outwardly, building careers, forming relationships, and establishing social identity (the *persona*).

However, midlife often brings internal unease, a feeling that previous goals no longer satisfy. Jung described this process as *individuation*, an inward journey towards integrating previously hidden or undeveloped aspects of oneself.

Clients often enter coaching with seemingly practical questions: 'Should I retire?' or 'What's next?' but these questions mask deeper themes: identity, purpose, legacy, and mortality. Jung's insights help coaches appreciate these underlying psychological transitions. Our role is to create space for clients to explore, aligning their outward choices with inner realities. Meaning and maturity often emerge because of, not in spite of, ageing.

Erik Erikson and lifespan development

Erik Erikson's psychosocial theory provides a helpful lens for understanding midlife and later-life transitions. He outlined a series of developmental tasks across the lifespan. In midlife (defined in his time as approximately ages 40–65), the central tension is *generativity versus stagnation*, the desire to contribute meaningfully through mentoring, creating, volunteering, or leaving a legacy. When this drive is unmet, individuals may experience stagnation, emptiness, burnout, or dissatisfaction.

In later life, Erikson described the task of *ego integrity versus despair*, typically beginning around age 65. This involves reflecting on life's meaning and coherence. Integrity emerges from making peace with the past and embracing the life one has lived; despair stems from unresolved regrets or a sense that life has been wasted.

Yet in today's longer, more fluid lives, these stages often shift. The traditional endpoint of 65 no longer feels like the threshold to despair. Many people now continue seeking purpose, growth, and contribution well into their 70s and beyond. For some, deep reflection and reckoning with life's meaning may not surface until their 80s. This delay doesn't negate Erikson's insights; it reflects how our psychological development continues to evolve alongside changing social patterns, health expectations, and longevity.

This shift in how we view our lives over time is supported by a growing body of research into what's known as the 'Happiness Curve'.

The happiness curve: Why ageing might surprise you

It might sound counterintuitive, but research suggests we actually get happier as we age. Jonathan Rauch's book *The Happiness Curve* (2018) explores how life satisfaction dips in midlife, often due to unmet expectations, comparison, and invisible pressures, but gradually rises again in later years. This U-shaped curve of wellbeing has been observed across cultures, income levels, and even personality types.

Why does happiness increase with age? Because we start letting go of what doesn't matter. We stop chasing external validation. We become better at appreciating the present, accepting imperfection, and valuing relationships and meaning over status or stuff.

This research challenges outdated assumptions about ageing as decline. It reminds us, and our clients, that later life isn't just something to cope with; it can be a time to flourish.

In career coaching, these developmental tasks are not abstract concepts. Clients may wrestle with generativity, longing to contribute meaningfully, or they may revisit earlier identity questions as life circumstances change. Others may begin to reflect more seriously on legacy or grapple with late-emerging regrets. Coaches must recognise and honour these deeper psychological layers, creating space for clients to articulate what still matters, clarify the contributions they still wish to make, and find coherence and contentment in life's unfolding later chapters.

Retirement as revivement or re-tyrement

The word 'retirement' suggests withdrawal. But many clients today are looking for something very different. I sometimes refer to this stage as 'revivement', or even 're-tyrement', a metaphorical change of tyres rather than a full stop. Just as tyres are changed for different terrains, clients seek new kinds of traction, momentum, and fulfilment. Reframing retirement helps clients view this transition not as an end but as a new beginning.

Navigating emotional and practical realities

Clients may experience this transition as liberating or unsettling. Some feel creativity, excitement, and possibility; others wrestle with grief, loss, or uncertainty. Loss of a professional role can raise profound questions about self-worth. Health issues or caregiving responsibilities can dramatically alter life priorities, sometimes forcing difficult trade-offs between work, personal goals, and family responsibilities.

Yet this stage of life also holds great potential. Many clients discover new interests, passions, and ways to contribute, finally gaining the freedom to pursue long-held dreams. Coaching at this stage must consider both emotional and practical dimensions. It involves exploring evolving identities, clarifying values, and redefining a sense of purpose. The coach becomes a trusted partner, not merely facilitating goals but accompanying clients in this deeper exploration.

Why career coaching must evolve

While traditional career coaching, focused on career discovery, CVs, interviews, and job search, remains important, it's no longer sufficient for clients navigating later-life transitions. Coaching at this stage benefits from a broader understanding of identity, transition, and meaning-making.

Effective coaches in this area need comfort with uncertainty and ambiguity. They must skilfully listen for both expressed and unexpressed client needs and explore questions that may not have immediate or obvious answers.

Midlife and retirement coaching is inherently holistic. It draws from career development theories, adult psychology, narrative practices, and life-design frameworks, respecting the client's full life context rather than just career issues. This book provides tools and insights to support such an integrated, comprehensive approach, recognising career transitions after age 50 as deeply personal journeys rather than mere professional decisions.

What this book offers

This book is written for trained career professionals who want to deepen their expertise with clients aged 50 and above. Whether your clients are navigating the later stages of working life, contemplating retirement, or simply wondering what comes next, you'll find practical frameworks, reflective exercises, and language to support meaningful conversations. Individuals in this age group may also find it a helpful guide as they reflect on their own transitions.

You won't find detailed financial planning advice here, though money matters inevitably arise in coaching. Instead, the focus is on helping clients align their choices with their values, energy, and aspirations as they move through change.

Health is another critical factor, often emerging unexpectedly. Patrick, an HGV mechanic, faced a triple bypass and needed a phased return to work. Instead, his employer expected him back full-time, adding stress to an already precarious situation. I too experienced a significant health setback, a concussion that required several months of recovery. My flexible career made that healing possible, but not everyone has that kind of freedom.

Midlife and later-life career coaching isn't about giving answers. It's about creating space for exploration, reflection, and clarity – helping people recalibrate their priorities, navigate uncertainty, and make choices that feel right for them.

As a coach, you are a trusted companion on that journey. This book is here to support you, offering structure without rigidity, guidance without prescription, and a human-centred approach to the evolving landscape of later life.

We are not preparing people to retire from life, but to step into the next chapter with insight and purpose.

In a nutshell

- Longer lives and shifting retirement patterns are reshaping career transitions beyond midlife, requiring new coaching approaches.

- Identity, purpose, and contribution in later life are important. (Drawing on psychological theories from Jung and Erikson.)

- Effective later-life coaching involves not just tools, but presence, curiosity, and the ability to hold space for uncertainty and possibility.

Chapter 2
Understanding midlife career transitions

> **Summary**
>
> *Midlife career change is rarely simple. It's shaped by identity, values, and life stage, not just ambition or opportunity. This chapter explores the emotional and psychological landscape of midlife transitions, including confidence, mindset, and control. We'll introduce practical coaching tools and share real-life stories to help you support clients navigating this rich, complex, and often deeply personal terrain.*

Introduction

Midlife career transitions are different. They rarely follow the structured, linear path we associate with earlier career stages. Not the straightforward path from education to first job or the typical route to becoming a chartered professional. Instead, they are often complex, emotionally charged, and deeply personal.

While early career decisions may be shaped by ambition, external expectations, or financial necessity, midlife brings a different lens. At this stage, people begin to ask deeper questions: Is this it? What now? Who am I now? What do I want from the next phase of life? What kind of work, or life, feels worth doing? What legacy do I want to leave?

This internal reflection can be triggered by dissatisfaction at work, a change in life circumstances, or the dawning sense that time ahead is less than time already lived.

What complicates these transitions further is the reorientation of values. What once mattered – status, salary, recognition – may no longer hold the same weight. Instead, clients increasingly seek work that aligns with who they are now, not who they were. The shift is not just about employment but about identity, purpose, and what matters most at this stage of life.

Career decisions in midlife are often less about climbing and more about meaning, wellbeing, and identity. But not always.

Some, like Sarah (from Chapter 1), are still driven by growth, momentum, and entrepreneurial ambition, building businesses, seeking promotions, or making bold sideways moves. In contrast, others are pausing to re-evaluate. Take David, 58, who recently stepped back from a senior role after a health scare. For him, this stage isn't about scaling up; it's about reclaiming time, reconnecting with family, and exploring work that feels purposeful but less consuming.

The key is recognising that midlife is not one homogenous phase. Someone at 50 and someone at 65 may have very different priorities, circumstances, and energy levels. Indeed, two people at 60 could have very different goals. What matters is not just their age, but the stage they are at in life.

The landscape of midlife career change

The triggers for career change in midlife are varied and often layered. For some, it's the external jolt of redundancy or organisational restructuring. For others, it's a slower internal shift; a quiet restlessness, or the growing sense that what once fit no longer does.

Midlife clients often describe reaching a crossroads. Some speak of plateauing in roles they've mastered. Others reach a crisis point after burnout, a health scare, or the death of a loved one, events that prompt deeper reflection on how they spend their time and energy. These transitions are rarely driven by a single factor. More often, they arise from a complex interplay of life experience, evolving values, and changing priorities.

As coaches, we can help clients acknowledge this complexity and explore a future that aligns with their current identity, energy, and aspirations.

I've seen this shift in countless clients and experienced it myself. At midlife, we begin to reassess not just *what* we want from work but *why*. We become more aware of time and more motivated to use it well.

Despite the skills and potential of people aged 50 and beyond, many still face ageism, outdated stereotypes, or rigid systems that fail to reflect their value. Culturally, we are still catching up. Most organisations are not designed to accommodate the evolving needs and ambitions of midlife workers. There remains an assumption of decline or winding down, rather than renewal or reinvention.

And yet, many in their 50s and 60s are entering a new, dynamic phase of life, with clarity, capability, and energy. Let's share some stories from Heather, Mark, and Joe.

HEATHER, 56: RECLAIMING PURPOSE AFTER FEELING OVERLOOKED

Despite a successful career in STEM, Heather came to coaching feeling increasingly sidelined. Younger colleagues were being fast-tracked while her development stalled. 'It's like they stopped seeing my potential', she said. Coaching gave her space to re-evaluate not just how to stay employed but how to align her work with her values. Heather transitioned into a part-time consultancy role and began mentoring women in STEM, reconnecting with her original sense of purpose.

Coaching reflection: Clients may need help reframing what's been lost so they can recognise what they're moving towards. Later-life roles often prioritise congruence over status.

MARK, 61: CHOOSING CONTRIBUTION OVER CLIMBING

Mark had always been ambitious. After redundancy, he surprised himself by not wanting to chase another senior position. Instead, he felt drawn to contribute in a quieter way. He started volunteering with a youth mentoring programme, supporting young people on the margins of education. The work lit him up. Eventually, he accepted a part-time role supporting financial literacy workshops.

'I used to define success by my title', he said. 'Now it's about what I leave behind.'

Coaching reflection: Contribution, not advancement, often becomes the driver in the second half of life.

JOE, 54: FEELING 'TOO OLD TO START AGAIN, TOO YOUNG TO STOP'

Joe's technical role was eliminated as automation took hold. At 54, he felt in limbo: not old enough to retire but unsure how to start something new. He felt the ground had shifted beneath him. In coaching, he reflected on what he still loved, explaining things, breaking down processes, helping others succeed. That led to a new direction: training apprentices. He became a mentor and coach, using his technical knowledge in a fresh way.

Coaching reflection: Midlife transitions can open up roles that feel more meaningful, especially those rooted in guidance and support.

The emotional and psychological journey

Career change in midlife is rarely just a practical move; it's a psychological shift. Letting go of a long-held role or identity can provoke grief, anxiety, and vulnerability, even when the decision is voluntary.

Clients often grapple with deep-seated fears: Am I too old to start again? Who would want to hire me now? In ageist environments, some feel invisible, others uncertain or diminished. These emotional responses must be acknowledged before practical solutions can take root.

> **Like bad dating: The emotional toll of modern job search**
>
> For many over 50, looking for work today can feel less like a professional exchange and more like an emotional minefield. Ghosting. Automated rejections. Weeks of silence after final interviews. Vague promises of follow-up that never arrive. It's easy to start wondering, *Is it me?*
>
> The process mirrors bad dating: you're left waiting, unsure where you stand, and second-guessing what you said or did. But unlike dating, this isn't just about feelings; it affects your income, identity, and confidence.
>
> Many organisations behave like untrustworthy partners: not responding, keeping candidates in limbo, or making decisions without transparency. For midlife candidates who grew up in a world where professionalism included courtesy and follow-through, this shift can be deeply disorienting.
>
> Help clients to remember: this isn't personal, even when it feels that way. The system is broken, not you. Holding onto your self-respect and finding communities of support can make all the difference.

What complicates midlife transitions further is the reorientation of values. What once mattered – status, salary, recognition – may no longer hold the same weight. Instead, clients increasingly seek work that aligns with who they are now, not who they were. The shift is not just in employment, but in identity, purpose, and what matters most at this stage of life.

Chapter 2: Understanding Midlife Career Transitions

Coaching reflection: Supporting clients to define alignment in midlife

Many high-performing clients begin to feel a quiet dissonance in their roles as they enter their 50s and beyond, a subtle mismatch between their current work and who they've become. As a coach, your role is to help surface and explore this shift with curiosity and strategic focus.

Use the following prompts to guide reflective discussion or journalling between sessions:

- What kinds of challenges does your client now feel motivated to address?
- How has their leadership style evolved, and how do they want to be experienced by others?
- What types of conversations, cultures, or causes do they now find energising?
- What kinds of organisations or initiatives would they feel proud to be associated with?
- Where in their life or work are they already experiencing a sense of alignment, and what insights emerge from this?

These questions help clients move beyond dissatisfaction or restlessness and towards a clearer professional filter, one that informs repositioning, networking, and decision-making in a more values-led way.

Coaching takeaway: Naming what matters now

Use these prompts to help clients move from vague dissatisfaction to actionable clarity. When clients articulate what alignment looks like *now*, they're better equipped to evaluate opportunities, reposition their narrative, and make grounded decisions about what comes next.

As I've written elsewhere: It can be easy to focus on all the reasons why you won't get a job and that employers prefer youth. Sometimes we skip over more positive stories. Mindset matters. What we believe about ourselves shapes how we show up, and what becomes possible.

This is not about forced optimism, but about recognising the role of belief, self-talk, and emotional readiness. Tools such as visualisation, affirmations, and dialogue coaching aren't superficial; they're foundational. Helping clients identify and reframe their inner narratives can unlock forward movement.

Let's look at Richard, Rachel, and Anita.

RICHARD, 59: OVERCOMING A SELF-SABOTAGING MINDSET

Richard had been successful in finance, but post-redundancy, his inner critic was loud. 'Who would want someone my age?' he'd ask. He struggled to even send out his CV, convinced it would be ignored. In coaching, he explored where those beliefs had come from, early messages about being replaceable, shame around ageing, and fear of being irrelevant. He began rewriting his inner script, noticing his self-talk, and gently challenging it. Eventually, he reached out to a small firm in his network and was invited to lead a project on succession planning, turning his age into an advantage.

Coaching reflection: Reframing the inner critic can be the real turning point in later-life transitions.

RACHEL, 55: CALM DETERMINATION AND CAREER CLARITY

Rachel was methodical and grounded. After taking redundancy, she didn't panic or rush. Instead, she spent time clarifying what really mattered in her next role: values, flexibility, and a respectful team culture. She reached out to past colleagues, updated her professional profile, and pursued roles with quiet determination. In coaching, she explored not only skills but what she needed to thrive emotionally. Eventually, she joined a purpose-led startup that valued her experience without requiring constant hustle.

Coaching reflection: Emotional steadiness is a powerful asset in transition. It creates space for intentional decision-making.

ANITA, 60: REFRAMING IDENTITY AFTER STEPPING DOWN

Anita had built a senior leadership career in the charity sector. After stepping down, she felt not relief, but uncertainty. Without the title and inbox, her deeper identity felt exposed. Coaching helped her explore her values, energy sources, and the influence she still wanted. She took on a part-time consultancy role supporting smaller organisations. Not a step down, but a conscious realignment. She stopped introducing herself by her old title and began saying, 'I work with emerging leaders in the sector'.

Coaching reflection: Clients may need help reframing what they've left behind to recognise what they're stepping into. Later-life roles often prioritise congruence over status.

Coaching prompts: The emotional and psychological journey

This set of prompts supports clients in navigating the inner terrain of later-life transitions. Use them to explore identity, values, confidence, and the stories people carry about ageing, all of which shape their sense of purpose and possibility.

- What have you had to let go of in this transition, and what are you beginning to reclaim?
- How have your values shifted over time, and how might they shape your next steps?
- What story are you currently telling yourself about your age, abilities, or future, and whom does that story serve?
- When do you feel most confident or purposeful? What patterns do you notice?
- Are there parts of your identity you want to bring forward more fully in your next chapter?
- What limiting beliefs might be holding you back, and how could you begin to challenge them?
- If you were to imagine your next chapter as a positive turning point, what would it look and feel like?

Confidence, locus of control, and mindset

Confidence

A dip in confidence is one of the most common consequences of redundancy or role loss in midlife. Even clients with long, successful careers can feel destabilised by the sudden loss of structure, identity, and professional validation. Their belief in themselves may be shaken. They begin to question their relevance, skills, and future value, especially in a labour market that often overvalues youth and overlooks experience.

Some clients interpret redundancy as a personal failure rather than an organisational decision. They may carry internalised shame or embarrassment, which inhibits action and makes it difficult to speak confidently about their achievements.

This is where coaching can make a tangible difference. Helping clients reframe what's happened, and what it means, can rebuild self-esteem. We can guide them to explore what remains strong, not just what's been lost. Normalising the emotional impact of redundancy, while gently challenging harsh self-judgements, is often a first step towards forward movement.

Locus of control

It's also important to pay close attention to a client's locus of control, their beliefs about what they can and cannot influence. Clients with an *internal locus of control* tend to believe their actions matter. They're more likely to take initiative, adapt to change, and interpret setbacks as learning opportunities. In contrast, those with an *external locus of control* may feel things happen *to* them. They can feel powerless, resigned, or overly dependent on the decisions of others.

Clients with a strong external locus might say things like:

> 'No one wants someone my age.'
> 'It's all about who you know.'
> 'There's nothing I can do.'

In these cases, coaching can focus on rebuilding agency, not by denying difficult realities, but by identifying small, achievable actions that restore a sense of control. Encouraging experimentation, curiosity, and reflection, such as trying out new roles, reconnecting with dormant networks, or learning a skill, can gradually shift their mindset towards possibility.

Mindset and self-talk

Mindset plays a pivotal role in midlife career transitions. Many clients internalise limiting beliefs such as:

> 'I'm too old.'
> 'They won't hire someone like me.'
> 'My best years are behind me.'

These thoughts often go unchallenged, yet they quietly shape expectations, energy, and outcomes. Left unchecked, they can become a self-fulfilling prophecy.

As coaches, we help clients uncover and question these inner narratives, and develop more constructive ones. Practical tools such as visualisation and affirmations (see the section 'Positive affirmations and visualisation' later in this chapter) can support this process. Encouraging clients to imagine success, reflect on their value, or post daily affirmations like: *'I am skilled and experienced, and my age is an asset'* can lead to subtle but meaningful shifts in outlook.

Phil, a client, captured this well:

> *I needed to shift the balance between the positive, focused, effective thoughts and the draining, destructive ones. The intentional ones can be tweaked; the unintentional take on a life of their own, like weeds in a garden.*

His metaphor is a reminder that managing mindset isn't about perfection; it's about tending to our thoughts with awareness and care. Helping clients strengthen empowering beliefs, *I bring experience* rather than *I'm too old*, isn't about wishful thinking. It's about cultivating the mindset that enables real action, resilience, and results.

JAMES, 62: REBUILDING AGENCY THROUGH SMALL ACTIONS

James had worked for the same engineering company for 25 years. When the site closed, he was stunned. The routines, relationships, and role he'd relied on were gone. In coaching, he was invited to take micro-steps: attend a webinar, reconnect with a colleague, update his CV. Each action felt manageable. With time, these steps shifted his sense of self, from discarded employee to someone navigating his future. Eventually, he took on a part-time project management role and began mentoring junior staff. His confidence returned, slowly but surely.

Coaching reflection: Rebuilding agency doesn't require a leap, just the courage to take the next small step.

LINA, 59: FINDING CONFIDENCE THROUGH CONNECTION

Lina had burned out. After leaving a demanding health role, she withdrew unsure what was next, lacking confidence, and feeling invisible. Her world had shrunk. Her coach invited her to take one small step: invite a friend for coffee. That conversation reminded her of her strengths. From there, she volunteered, then reconnected with former colleagues. She began mentoring in a community health project. Each small step restored her confidence. She didn't need a full plan, just a way back to herself.

Coaching reflection: Connection often precedes clarity. Confidence is rebuilt through relational affirmation.

To help clients rebuild confidence and regain a sense of agency, the following tools can be particularly effective.

COACHING TOOL 2.1: Confidence tracker

Purpose: Helps clients visualise fluctuations in their confidence over time and identify what boosts or drains it.

How to use:

Ask the client to keep a simple weekly log, noting:

- confidence level (1–10) at the start and end of the week;
- what increased their confidence;
- what undermined it;
- what they did that gave them energy or agency.

Example table:

Week	Level (1–10)	Confidence boosters	Confidence drainers	Key actions taken
1	4 → 5	Spoke to ex-colleague; updated CV	Comparing self to others on LinkedIn	Sent 1 application; called ex-manager
2	5 → 7	Completed online course	No response from recruiter	Reached out to 2 new contacts

As a coach, you can reflect on these patterns with the client.

Coaching question: *What consistently lifts you? How can we increase that? What can you let go of or reframe?*

COACHING TOOL 2.2: Control wheel

Purpose: Helps clients distinguish between what they can control, can influence, and what's outside their control.

How to use:

Draw three concentric circles labelled:

- **Inner circle:** *What I can control* (e.g. my CV, mindset, daily routine).
- **Middle circle:** *What I can influence* (e.g. networking, how others perceive me).
- **Outer circle:** *What I can't control* (e.g. ageist hiring policies, economic shifts).

Coaching question: 'Where are you spending most of your energy right now? How can we shift more attention to the inner circles?'
You can also prompt clients to write 'post-its' or phrases onto each section to externalise thoughts and increase clarity.

Using these tools with clients

CATHY, 55: REBUILDING CONFIDENCE AFTER FEELING STUCK AND INVISIBLE

Cathy had left her NHS role after a period of intense stress. She wanted to work again but felt emotionally fragile. Her energy fluctuated. She worried she wouldn't cope. In coaching, Cathy tracked her energy and confidence across a typical week using these two tools. She spotted patterns: when she felt strongest and what drained her. This gave her permission to design a week with space and structure. She applied for a part-time advisory role, one she might have dismissed before. She now describes herself as 'more grounded than ever'.

Coaching reflection: Externalising energy and confidence helps clients see their patterns and rebuild capacity realistically.

HENRYK, 60: FINDING PURPOSE AFTER REDUNDANCY AND LOW CONFIDENCE

Henryk had been laid off after decades in logistics. He felt flat, as if all momentum had vanished. In coaching, he talked about the quiet shame he felt: 'I never imagined being let go this late in life.' Exploring strengths helped shift the focus. He realised he still enjoyed organising, problem-solving, and supporting others.

Through a friend, he began doing freelance support for a contractor and found the work satisfying. The label of redundancy didn't define him; his actions did.

Coaching reflection: Later-life work may emerge through trust-based referrals, not just applications. Strength-based reflection can unlock direction.

Coaching prompts: Confidence, locus of control, and mindset

Use these prompts to support clients facing uncertainty, shifting identity, or loss of confidence in later life. They explore evolving narratives, definitions of success, and the emotional demands of transition.

- What is this transition asking of you, emotionally, practically, or psychologically?
- How do you currently define success, and how has that definition evolved over time?
- What part of your identity feels most impacted by this career shift?
- Are there any narratives (your own or others') that you might need to challenge in this phase?
- How are your health, energy, and life stage influencing your career and life decisions right now?

Cultural and contextual influences

Midlife transitions are never just about age. They are shaped by class, culture, gender, ethnicity, and personal history. These factors influence how people perceive their options, define success, and approach change.

For instance, someone from a working-class background may have had fewer educational opportunities, limiting their early career choices and shaping beliefs about what's realistic. Financial pressures, such as supporting family or lacking pension savings, may restrict their ability to explore or take risks. In contrast, clients with greater social capital or financial freedom may feel more emboldened to experiment, retrain, or pursue personal interests.

A client who has spent years as a full-time carer may question their employability, despite having developed advanced relational, organisational, and emotional skills. Others may carry cultural expectations about retirement, ambition, or gender roles that subtly shape what they feel is *allowed*.

These factors may not be named explicitly in coaching, but they show up in self-talk, decision-making, and imagined futures. Coaches need to tune into these contextual layers with cultural humility and curiosity. That means noticing unconscious bias, surfacing assumptions, and exploring the life scripts that guide a client's sense of possibility.

Understanding what success looks like through the client's cultural lens can uncover both hidden fears and latent ambitions.

Let's look at some examples:

AYESHA, 59: BALANCING CULTURAL EXPECTATIONS WITH CREATIVE WORK

Ayesha, a British Asian woman, wanted to leave her senior NHS role but felt torn between cultural expectations of stability and her desire to work more creatively. Through coaching, she gave herself permission to explore a more flexible, freelance path in health education.

Coaching reflection: Clients may need support to honour both cultural expectations and personal aspirations, especially when choosing creativity or flexibility over traditional stability.

MARTIN, 58: REFRAMING REDUNDANCY

Martin had left school at 16 and worked his way up in manufacturing. Being made redundant felt like failure. 'I promised myself I'd always provide.' In coaching, he explored the story he carried about class, success, and being a provider. Gradually, he reframed redundancy not as an end, but as a shift. He found a role with a smaller company closer to home, with better balance. 'It's not less. It's different.'

Coaching reflection: Social narratives around class, work, and masculinity often shape meaning-making. Reframing is a powerful act of liberation.

ELENA, 61: REDISCOVERING SKILLS AFTER CARING

Elena had cared full-time for her mother for several years. After her mother's death, she felt untethered, unsure of her place or skills. Through coaching, she began to map the emotional intelligence, planning, and boundary-setting she'd developed during caregiving. She realised she'd gained more than she'd lost.

She later trained as a life coach, drawing on her lived experience to support others in transition.

Coaching reflection: Caring roles are often invisible but rich in transferable strengths and insight. Naming these can restore confidence and agency.

Retirement on the horizon

As people approach their late 50s and 60s, retirement becomes part of the mental landscape, even for those who have no intention of stopping work any time soon. There's often a subtle shift in perspective, from *What's next?* to *How do I want to spend the rest of my life?*

The concept of retirement starts to influence how clients evaluate future roles. Some begin to look for bridge jobs or phased exit strategies. Others want to pivot to something more flexible, creative, or purpose-driven, viewing retirement not as a cliff edge, but as a transition. A growing number no longer resonate with the idea of a fixed retirement age. They want to stay active and engaged, but on their own terms. And there are some who want one more 'big job' or a final reach to a high-level position.

Clients may want to downshift or reduce hours. Some seek encore careers. Others want to give back, pursue long-postponed interests, or finally prioritise wellbeing over ambition. So many clients, so many possibilities.

As coaches, we can help clients frame retirement not as an ending, but as an evolving transition, one that can include a mix of work, leisure, learning, contribution, and rest.

Helping clients reflect on their desired lifestyle, income needs, health, and sense of meaning can lead to more sustainable, satisfying decisions. The 'next chapter' is not about withdrawal, but rebalancing.

As I wrote in *Rethinking Retirement for Positive Ageing*: *The transition from work to retirement can take several years to conclude. It is a subjective journey involving a psychosocial transition rather than a single event.*

This process often unfolds in three stages:

1. **Pre-retirement:** reflection and planning;
2. **Transition:** experimentation, adjustment, occasional stress; and
3. **Adjustment:** stabilising into a new rhythm of life.

Clients like Henryk often need support navigating this liminal space. While he could have simply retired, he chose instead to engage in a series of coaching conversations that helped him explore what mattered most and to design a transition filled with purpose, flexibility, and autonomy.

Retirement, then, isn't about stopping work; it's about reimagining how work, time, and meaning will shape the next chapter.

> **COACHING TOOL 2.3: Three coaching questions to reframe retirement**
>
> This mini-framework supports clients in shifting from a narrow view of retirement as 'the end of work' to a more open, purpose-led transition. It works especially well with clients who are unsure what they want next, or who feel anxious about 'what comes after'.
>
> 1. **What does *retirement* mean to you: culturally, emotionally, practically?**
>   Many people inherit assumptions about retirement (rest, withdrawal, decline) that no longer fit. This question helps surface unspoken beliefs and opens the door to reframing.
>
> 2. **What role do you want work, contribution, or purpose to play in your life over the next 5–10 years?**
>   Encourages clients to think holistically. This might include paid work, volunteering, mentoring, or creative pursuits.
>
> 3. **If retirement were a creative project, not a financial deadline, what would you design?**
>   This question shifts the energy from obligation to possibility. It invites clients to imagine retirement not as a shutdown but as an unfolding.
>
> **And also:**
> Invite clients to sketch their 'ideal week' five years from now. What's included? What's absent? This often reveals hidden priorities and longings.

Health, energy, and unexpected life events

Midlife transitions don't happen in a vacuum. This stage of life brings physical, emotional, and practical realities that can't be ignored. A decline in energy, the onset of chronic conditions, or caring responsibilities for ageing parents or ill partners can reshape what's possible, or what's desirable.

Sometimes clients are forced to step back, not because they want to, but because they can't see any alternative. They may leave a job to move across the country and care for a parent, or reduce their hours due to their own health needs. Others are pushed back into work after unexpected life events: divorce, bereavement, or, as happened with one client, the shock of discovering that their partner has run up a substantial financial loss, resulting in the sale of their home and long-term plans being changed.

These situations profoundly impact how clients view work, time, and what matters most.

Some clients feel a new urgency to act while they still can. Others become more risk-averse, preferring security and routine over reinvention. Coaches can help clients assess their energy levels realistically and explore how to structure work around life, not the other way around.

It's not just about roles and CVs; it's about capacity, grief, resilience, and renewal.

One client, Jim, found himself managing multiple transitions at once: redundancy, the end of a long-term relationship, a sudden housing change, and ongoing health recovery. Ideally, we deal with one big life change at a time, but life doesn't always cooperate. Jim described the experience as *'like spinning too many plates and dropping most of them'*. In coaching, we slowed everything down and focused on stabilisation before goal-setting. That act of pausing, of creating space to breathe, became the turning point.

Another client, Carla, had left her job abruptly to care for her mother with dementia. She returned four years later feeling unemployable, despite decades of senior experience. Coaching helped her reconnect with her skills, reframe her caregiving role as a strength, and eventually transition into a part-time advisory role in the same sector.

Coaches must support clients to prioritise wellbeing, plan realistically, and honour their emotional state. Even the most capable individuals can struggle when hit by too much at once. Our role is to meet them with empathy and flexibility, offering not just strategy, but stability.

MARIA, 57: PAUSING TO RESET

Maria came to coaching while juggling part-time work and caring for her mother with dementia. 'I used to be on top of everything', she said, 'but now I'm constantly behind and guilty about all of it'. She wasn't lacking ability; she was emotionally and physically depleted.

Rather than push for quick decisions, coaching focused first on her wellbeing: building space to reflect, rest, and gradually reimagine what was possible. Over time, Maria shaped a more realistic plan, scaling back work and exploring flexible roles. What she valued most wasn't a list of goals; it was having space to feel steady and seen again.

Coaching reflection: Sometimes the most powerful step is pausing. Coaching can offer a steady space to rest, reflect, and reset before reimagining what's next.

Job loss as a form of grief

Job loss can evoke emotions remarkably similar to those experienced in bereavement: shock, anger, sadness, disbelief, and even shame. For many in midlife, a job is more than a source of income; it represents structure, identity, and value. Recognising the grief-like nature of job loss can help clients make sense of their emotional response and begin the process of healing.

Coaching prompts: Health, energy, and unexpected life events

These prompts help clients process the emotional impact of endings, disruptions, and losses. They encourage meaning-making and gentle rituals to support healing and transition.

- What feelings came up when your job ended, and which ones surprised you?
- How would you name or describe the loss you've experienced?
- Are there any rituals, symbols, or practices (e.g. journaling, photography, goodbye letters) that might help you mark this transition?

Redefining success in midlife

One of the most liberating aspects of midlife is the opportunity to redefine what success means. No longer constrained by earlier definitions of achievement, many clients begin to seek:

- less stressful roles in the same field;
- a shift to a portfolio or freelance career;
- time to explore a long-held interest or creative pursuit;
- a return to study or voluntary work; and
- flexibility and meaning over status.

The notion of a zigzag or lateral move becomes not only acceptable but desirable. Success is increasingly defined by impact, balance, joy, or contribution rather than job title or salary band.

As one client put it: *I've had the job with the car and the salary. Now I want the work that fits me.*

Others arrive in coaching without a clear vision. This reflects what Hudson (1999) describes as *regressive* versus *generative* transitions, the former driven by safety, the latter by reflection and growth.

Some clients may initially opt for a regressive transition, choosing something safe and familiar. Sophie, for example, accepted a similar role after redundancy, knowing it wasn't quite right. A year later, she returned to coaching, ready to make a more values-led decision.

In contrast, generative transitions emerge when clients take time to reflect on what matters most. Paul spent several months exploring his interests and energy levels before transitioning into part-time consultancy and volunteer mentoring, combining impact with balance.

Understanding the difference between reactive and intentional choices is a key coaching role. Clients often need help to slow down, reconnect with their evolving identity, and define success on their own terms.

For much of my life, success meant financial security and professional reputation. But that's changed. These days, success feels more like having time to simply *be*. I still enjoy my work, especially research and writing, but I also need space to walk in the woods, to notice the shift in seasons, and to literally stop and smell the world around me.

AMINA, 58: EMBRACING A MORE FLEXIBLE, FULFILLING PATH

Amina had spent her entire career in local government and assumed she'd continue until retirement. But after taking leave to support her daughter through a difficult pregnancy, her perspective shifted. 'I didn't realise how much of myself I'd put on hold', she said. Coaching gave her space to reconsider what she wanted from work and life. Instead of returning full-time, she took a role coordinating community projects at a local school. It paid less but gave her more flexibility, connection, and joy. 'It wasn't the plan', she reflected, 'but it feels like the right kind of success for now'.

Coaching reflection: Midlife transitions often invite clients to redefine success. Coaching can help surface what truly matters: flexibility, joy, and a life more aligned with the self.

> **Coaching tip:**
>
> Coaches can help clients reframe these paths as progress, not retreat. The ladder may no longer be the goal. The journey itself becomes the achievement.

The coach's role

Coaching at this stage is not about pushing clients to do more or go faster; it's about transformation. It's about holding space for grief, reinvention, and uncertainty. It means challenging unhelpful narratives (*I'm too old*) while helping clients stay grounded in possibility.

The role of the coach becomes less about performance and more about permission: permission to pause, reflect, dream, and begin again.

Clients in midlife often need:

- a reflective space to untangle complex emotions;
- support to navigate grief, fear, or ambiguity;
- encouragement to reimagine, not just reapply;
- tools to challenge limiting beliefs; and
- realistic support to experiment and take action.

As Bruce Feiler (2021) writes, we all experience *life-quakes* that shake up our stories. Midlife is when many of those quakes converge. Coaches become companions in the process of reshaping identity, purpose, and direction.

Key roles of the coach include:

- validating the complexity of transition;
- helping clients surface and reframe internalised age-related beliefs;
- offering tools to explore values, purpose, and vision;
- supporting practical steps without rushing the process; and
- encouraging new narratives of growth, creativity, and contribution in later life.

> ### SUZANNE, 53: REBUILDING WITH BELIEF, BALANCE, AND INTENTION
>
> One client, Suzanne, said: 'Having chosen to take redundancy at 53, I agree that having a positive mindset is crucial. I needed to believe it was the right time for a shift, because no one else was going to believe it for me.' Suzanne was proactive but cautious. Coaching gave her the structure to explore new possibilities without the pressure to have it all figured out. She eventually moved into part-time consultancy alongside community-based work, creating a balance that suited both her values and her energy.
>
> **Coaching reflection:** Clients like Suzanne often need space to rebuild belief, not just plans. Coaching supports intentional choices rooted in energy, values, and self-trust.

Positive affirmations and visualisation

Just as athletes use mental rehearsal to prepare for performance, clients navigating transition can benefit from visualisation and affirmations. These techniques aren't superficial; they're mindset-shifting tools that support confidence, clarity, and resilience.

Affirmations like:

- I bring a lifetime of experience that matters.
- I am skilled, adaptable, and ready for the next chapter.
- I may be older, but I'm wiser, and I still have more to give.

Encouraging clients to write, speak, or even record their affirmations can help them override internalised narratives of decline. It may feel awkward at first, but these small scripts, repeated often, can gradually reshape self-perception.

Visualisation exercises might involve imagining:

- themselves in a new role where they feel valued;
- a positive interview experience; and
- a '*day in the life*' five years from now, doing work they love on terms they choose.

These techniques create a bridge between possibility and action, helping clients embody belief before it becomes reality. Let's make it real with a couple of stories.

CARLA, 55: VISUALISING CONFIDENCE

Carla had spent years caring for her partner, stepping away from work and gradually losing confidence. Returning felt daunting. I invited her to visualise herself at interview: calm, grounded, capable. She practised answering questions aloud and pictured herself with warmth. In her next interview, she felt steadier. Even her body language changed.

Coaching reflection: When clients can see and feel their future selves, belief often follows. Visualisation is not wishful thinking; it's mental rehearsal.

TOMASZ, 61: REBUILDING BELIEF THROUGH AFFIRMATIONS

Tomasz had worked in academia for most of his life. Post-retirement, he felt invisible. 'It's like I disappeared overnight', he said. In coaching, he began noticing his self-talk: 'I'm irrelevant', 'No one needs me now.' He started replacing these with quiet affirmations: 'I still have something to offer.' 'My voice matters.' Over time, these weren't just words; they became anchors. He joined a research network as a volunteer mentor.

Coaching reflection: Small shifts in language can recalibrate internal worlds. Affirmations give the brain new paths to walk.

Closing reflections

Midlife career transitions are layered. They involve the letting go of old identities, navigating fears about relevance, and embracing the possibility of reinvention. These transitions rarely emerge from ambition alone. More often, they arise from a deeper place, one rooted in values, meaning, and a desire to live with greater authenticity.

Midlife is not just about the loss of a role. It's about the redefinition of self. Identity, purpose, and contribution are all in motion. While the path forward may not be linear, it can be profoundly meaningful.

Clients often emerge from this process stronger, clearer, and more aligned with who they truly are. But this kind of transformation doesn't happen in isolation. It requires space, support, and a sense of psychological safety.

Midlife career transitions are not simply about changing jobs; they are about reshaping identity, rethinking purpose, and reclaiming agency. They call for coaches who can listen deeply, challenge gently, and hold a vision of what's possible, even when clients can't yet see it themselves.

As coaches, we are not just helping people find work. We're helping them reorient their lives.

With the right mindset, tools, and support, midlife can be one of the most creative and fulfilling chapters of all.

This work continues to move me. Time and again, I've seen clients navigate uncertainty and slowly reconnect with what matters. Coaching in midlife isn't about quick fixes or rushing into solutions. It's about creating space for reflection, for change, and sometimes for grief or surprise. It reminds us that ageing isn't decline; it's a process of unfolding. And when someone rediscovers purpose or shapes a life that fits who they are now, it confirms why this work is so important to me.

 In a nutshell

- Midlife is not one-size-fits-all, with diverse goals shaped by life stage, values, health, and identity.
- Mindset, self-talk, and locus of control influence action, confidence, and outcomes.
- Practical tools such as the Confidence Tracker and Control Wheel help build agency and clarity.
- Culture, caregiving, health, and retirement have an impact on career decision-making.
- The definition of success is evolving, as is the coach's role in supporting reflective, values-led choices.

Chapter 3
Coaching for career reinvention in midlife

> **Summary**
>
> *Reinvention at midlife is rarely a straight line. This chapter explores how to support clients navigating change with curiosity, courage, and clarity. From mindset shifts to personal branding, from skill translation to digital presence, we look at how coaches can help clients move from 'What now?' to a renewed sense of direction: one that fits who they are and what matters most now.*

The nature of career reinvention

Career reinvention in midlife doesn't always arrive in dramatic fashion. It's not always the big leap, the radical change, or the well-publicised pivot. More often, it emerges slowly, in the quiet realisation that the old version of working life no longer fits. For some, the catalyst is external: redundancy, burnout, a change in family structure, or financial necessity. For others, it's an internal shift: a desire for meaning, a yearning to do something more creative or impactful, or simply a need to live and work at a different pace.

What makes midlife career reinvention distinct is that it sits at the junction of personal history, accumulated experience, and future vision. Clients arrive in this phase with decades of life behind them: skills, relationships, successes, regrets, and stories. Unlike younger clients starting out, they are rarely trying to discover who they are. They are trying to decide who they want to become next.

Some reinventions are visible and bold: a corporate leader becomes a non-profit consultant; a teacher retrains as a coach. Others are subtler but equally profound: a client shifts from high-pressure project work to a part-time role that allows space for caregiving and creativity. Reinvention is not always a reinvention of identity. It can also be a realignment of values and energy.

As coaches, it's important to help clients name what's changing for them. Sometimes that shift is about the work itself, but more often, it's about how they want to *experience* work. They may no longer want to be the one leading the charge, managing people, or striving for promotions. Or they may, for the first time, feel a hunger to create, lead, or contribute on their own terms.

Clients often begin with vague statements like:

- 'I want to do something different, but I don't know what.'
- 'I'm not done yet; but I can't go on like this.'
- 'I want to matter, but in a different way now.'

These are not problems to be fixed, but invitations to explore. Reinvention, in midlife, is a developmental process as much as a professional one.

Reinvention is not just career change

It's important to differentiate reinvention from standard career change. Career change may involve a new job, a promotion, or a different employer. Career reinvention, on the other hand, often includes:

- a redefinition of identity;
- a reconsideration of priorities and values;
- a new relationship to time, energy, and contribution.

This deeper layer can take clients by surprise. They may expect to revise their CV, improve their interview skills, and land a new role within weeks. But underneath, they are also processing grief, questioning identity, and reshaping their vision for the future. Coaches who work at this level must be prepared to shift between the strategic and the reflective, to address the job search and the internal search in tandem.

A non-linear process

Reinvention in midlife is rarely linear. Clients may cycle through periods of enthusiasm and doubt, experimentation, and hesitation. Some begin a new direction, only to pause when caregiving demands arise or health issues intervene. Others take a *try before you commit* approach: freelancing, volunteering, or studying part-time to test the waters.

These shifts aren't signs of failure; they're signs of learning. Reinvention is iterative, not instantaneous. Helping clients see experimentation as progress reduces pressure and opens space for growth. One powerful approach is prototyping: small, low-risk experiments that allow clients to test new identities before fully committing.

JOANNA, 52: FROM REDUNDANCY TO REINVENTION

Joanna had spent years in retail management, a fast-paced and people-driven environment. When her store closed, she was made redundant. Rather than jump into another job, she took a course in psychology – something she'd always been curious about but had never explored. She became fascinated by wellbeing and community health. Over time, she began running local wellbeing sessions and eventually took on a part-time role with a mental health charity. The reinvention wasn't instant, but it was deeply her own.

Coaching reflection: Encouraging curiosity can be more powerful than pushing for clarity. Purpose often emerges through experimentation.

DEREK, 59: VOLUNTEERING AS A BRIDGE TO CHANGE

Derek worked in IT and had grown increasingly dissatisfied. The work felt routine, disconnected from what mattered. He started volunteering with a local wildlife group; something he'd loved in his youth. It brought him back to life. Through that, he began supporting their digital systems and eventually transitioned into a role combining tech and conservation. What began as a personal escape became a professional turning point.

Coaching reflection: Volunteering can be a low-risk entry into a new world; revealing values and sparking direction.

NATHAN, 56: 'I BUILT A CAREER IN A WORLD THAT'S DISAPPEARED'

Nathan had been a photo editor at a major fashion magazine for 18 years, loving the craft and artistry of the work. Then everything shifted: budget cuts, digital editing, AI-generated images. Eventually, he was made redundant. 'They wanted someone who could edit TikToks, not someone who knew lighting ratios', he said.

Coaching helped him mourn the *death of a craft* and explore adjacent paths. He began mentoring young photographers, launched a small archive of iconic fashion images, and was later invited to guest lecture at an art college. 'I stopped chasing trends', he said. 'Instead, I honoured what I know, and passed it on.'

Coaching reflection: When a client's world has changed beyond recognition, coaching can honour their legacy while opening new pathways for relevance and contribution.

Strategic positioning and personal branding

Career reinvention at midlife often requires a shift in how clients talk about themselves, and how others perceive them. After years or even decades in a single sector, role, or identity, clients can find it difficult to distil their value into a clear message that aligns with where they want to go next.

That's where strategic positioning and personal branding come in, not as superficial exercises in self-promotion, but as powerful tools for coherence, confidence, and connection.

Moving beyond the job title

Many clients have defined themselves by their job title: 'I'm a marketing director', 'I'm a teacher', 'I'm a solicitor'. But when they begin to reinvent, those titles may no longer fit, or may no longer open the right doors.

Coaches can help clients shift from role-based identity to value-based identity. That means focusing less on *what* they've done and more on *how they do it* and *what problems they solve*. It's the difference between saying:

- 'I was Head of Communications' versus 'I work with organisations to simplify complex ideas and make sure the right people hear them.' Or 'I help teams tell their story clearly, whether it's through campaigns, internal comms, or community engagement'.
- 'I worked in HR for 20 years' versus 'I help leaders navigate people decisions with empathy and clarity.' Or 'I bring experience in helping teams grow, resolve conflict, and build trust'.

This shift empowers clients to position themselves for future roles, rather than being boxed in by the past.

> **Coaching prompt: Rethinking identity beyond job titles**
>
> 'If you couldn't use your job title, how would you describe what you do and the difference you make?'
>
> *This prompt helps clients explore transferable skills, values, and personal impact beyond roles or sectors.*

To help clients translate this reflection into language and positioning, the following exercises can be useful.

> **COACHING TOOL 3.1: From title to value**
>
> **Step 1: Write down your most recent job title.**
>
> Then write two to three sentences describing:
>
> - what you actually did in that role;
> - what you were known for or proud of; and
> - what problems you helped solve.
>
> **Step 2: Now reframe it.**
>
> Without using your job title, write a new version that focuses on:
>
> - the value you bring;
> - the kind of impact you make; and
> - the way you approach your work.
>
> **Example template:**
>
> 'I help [who] do/achieve [what], by [how].'
> Encourage clients to test different phrases aloud and notice what feels most authentic. These can become the seeds of future bios, profiles, or networking conversations.

Reframing experience as a strength

Clients in midlife often carry internalised fears: that they're *too experienced*, *too expensive*, or *outdated*. These narratives can block opportunity before it's explored. Coaching can reframe this: experience brings calm under pressure, strategic thinking, and the ability to connect dots others might miss.

Coaches can help reframe this narrative: experience brings perspective, maturity, problem-solving depth, and reliability. The key is to own that value without sounding defensive.

A few reframing strategies

- **Position experience as calm clarity:**
  'I've encountered similar situations before and can quickly see what matters most.'
- **Highlight cross-sector adaptability with humility and perspective:**
  'I've worked across different areas, which helps me connect the dots and approach things with a fresh perspective.'
- **Use storytelling to build trust and relevance:**
  'That reminds me of a situation I worked through not long ago; here's how it unfolded.'

What matters is not just what they've done, but how it *translates* to what's needed now.

Crafting a personal brand story

A strong personal brand is not about slogans or logos. It's a coherent story: a line that connects a client's past to their desired future. It should reflect their values, strengths, and ambitions in a way that feels both true and strategic.

Coaches can guide clients through reflective exercises such as:

- What are the three words you want people to associate with you?
- What's the red thread that runs through all your roles?
- What motivates you now, and how has that evolved?

Encouraging clients to draft a short career narrative or positioning statement can be useful for interviews, networking, LinkedIn summaries, and conversations with potential collaborators.

The red thread: Finding coherence in later life

In reflective coaching, we sometimes speak of the *red thread*, a unifying theme that weaves through a person's life. It might be a core value, a deep longing, or a recurring role they've played. Even when life feels fragmented or non-linear, identifying this red thread can help people make sense of their choices, feel proud of what they've contributed, and shape the next chapter with renewed clarity.

ALEX, 58: FINDING THE THREAD THAT TIES IT ALL TOGETHER

When Alex first came to coaching, he described his career as a bit of a jumble, publishing, corporate training, consultancy. 'It's hard to explain what I do', he said, worried it looked scattered rather than strategic.

Branding work uncovered a clear thread: translating complex ideas into engaging learning experiences. His three brand words became clarity, creativity, and connection. Using these, we crafted a narrative showing how each chapter built on the last.

His new introduction:

> 'I design learning experiences that help people grow, whether in publishing, leadership development, or online education. I've always been about making ideas accessible and useful.'

Coaching reflection: Reframing a tangled work history into a cohesive story can shift not just how others see a client, but how they see themselves.

LENA, 53: MAKING IT WORK: REFRAMING A DECADE OF CARE

Lena had taken a 10-year break from formal employment to care for her children and later her father. 'I used to be a project manager, but now I just feel invisible', she said, worried the gap would overshadow everything else.

Coaching helped her recognise the skills she'd continued to use: organising, coordinating, advocating. She was still managing people, timelines, and complex logistics, just in a different context. Her brand words became organised, empathetic, and resourceful.

She crafted a positioning statement:

> 'I bring strong project and people coordination skills to roles that need calm under pressure and emotional intelligence. Whether in families or teams, I know how to make things work.'

Lena updated her LinkedIn profile and opened conversations about part-time roles in education and community health, spaces that aligned with her values.

Coaching reflection: Reframing life experience as skilled contribution helps clients like Lena move from feeling invisible to confidently owning their value.

Coaching prompt: Tracing the red thread

- What has quietly connected the different phases of your life, perhaps a value, curiosity, or way of being in the world?
- When you look back, what threads keep reappearing, even across different jobs, roles, or relationships?
- How might this thread guide you now?

Authenticity is key

Personal branding must feel real to be effective. Clients don't need to 'perform' a new identity, they need to articulate who they are becoming. This is especially important in midlife, where alignment and integrity matter more than ever.

A good brand communicates:

- *Clarity* (this is what I bring).
- *Credibility* (this is why I can do it).
- *Character* (this is how I show up).

When clients can own their story and speak from that place, they become more compelling, and more confident.

Coaching prompts: Strategic positioning and personal branding

These prompts support clients in reframing their experience, assumptions, and connections. They open up fresh ways to articulate value, explore future directions, and align work with wellbeing.

- What parts of your experience feel most relevant to where you want to go next?
- If you could reintroduce yourself professionally in one sentence, what would you say?
- What assumptions are you making about what employers or clients want from someone like you?
- How would working differently (e.g. flexibly, remotely, or for yourself) impact your energy, purpose, and wellbeing?
- Who might you reconnect with, or reach out to, that could open up new ideas or opportunities?

Translating skills and experience

One of the biggest challenges midlife clients face, especially those considering reinvention, is recognising and communicating the full value of their skills. After years in a single role, organisation, or sector, they may struggle to see how their experience transfers to something new. Some worry they're pigeonholed or that their past doesn't align with future goals. Others undervalue soft skills, informal learning, or experience gained outside of paid employment.

This is where coaching becomes invaluable. Helping clients connect the dots between what they've done and what's now possible is central to effective career reinvention.

Naming what's transferable

Clients often overlook the most powerful elements of their experience. They may say things like, 'I've only ever worked in education', or 'All I know is operations'. But when explored more deeply, their true value emerges: relationship building, process improvement, stakeholder communication, strategic thinking, mentoring, or problem-solving.

Coaches can help clients surface and name these skills by asking:

- What challenges have you solved repeatedly?
- What are you most proud of professionally?
- Where have you made things better, for people, systems, or outcomes?

Encourage a shift from tasks to capabilities:

- 'Managing a team' to developing others, handling conflict, performance coaching.
- 'Working in customer service' to problem-solving, de-escalation, relationship building.

From skills to story

It's not enough to list transferable skills; clients need to shape a narrative that shows how those skills apply in a new context. That story should include:

- what they've done;
- what they've learned; and
- how it equips them for what's next.

Use this simple **Career Story Prompt** to help clients shape a forward-facing narrative:

1. **Where have I been?**
   'I've worked in operational roles across logistics and supply chain for 25 years . . .'

2. **What's shifting?**
   '. . . but I've found myself more drawn to sustainability, process improvement, and values-led work.'

3. **Where am I going?**
   'Now I'm looking for roles in ethical supply chain management where I can apply my experience to support positive impact.'

This type of narrative helps recruiters, collaborators, and clients understand both the skills and the motivation behind a reinvention.

When experience doesn't fit the box

Some clients have experience that doesn't fit traditional categories, perhaps due to time out for caregiving, community work, or entrepreneurship. Others may feel dismissed because their path hasn't followed a straight line.

The coach's role is to frame the experience, so clients do not apologise for it. Clients with non-linear paths, caregiving breaks, or informal roles need help translating these into strengths, not just to prove value to others, but to reclaim it for themselves.

Examples:

- A full-time carer to emotional intelligence, planning, decision-making under pressure.
- A former small business owner to resourcefulness, client handling, financial literacy.
- A volunteer board member to governance insight, stakeholder negotiation, strategic input.

Beyond job titles: Reframing later-life presence

For many midlife clients, the traditional CV no longer tells the whole story. What matters now is how they show up: the values they bring, the way they work, and what energises them. Coaches can support clients to communicate this through personal branding, LinkedIn profiles, and conversations, moving from a list of past roles to a narrative of future potential.

Chapter 3: Coaching for Career Reinvention in Midlife

Coaching prompt: Learning from experience

'What did that experience teach you, and how does it apply to what you want next?'

This prompt encourages clients to extract insights from past experiences and apply them to future goals or transitions.

Creating age-inclusive workplaces: Insights from employers and over-60s

Research by Phoenix Insights (2024) reveals that many people over 60 feel uncertain about their future at work. Concerns about health, motivation, and age discrimination remain high, even as older workforce participation rises. Yet most employers still take a one-size-fits-all approach to development, overlooking the specific needs of later-life workers.

As career coaches, it's important to understand this broader landscape. HR leaders in the study called for more inclusive approaches, including:

- normalising later-life career transitions and returnships;
- flexible and phased work options;
- reskilling and mentoring pathways for midlife workers; and
- visibility of real-life stories to challenge ageist assumptions.

One contributor noted: *'For employees over 60, the workplace can feel like a crossroads.'* With tailored support, including coaching, this stage can become a pivot point, not an ending. Coaches can help clients:

- identify what support they need;
- practise conversations with employers; and
- assess whether workplace cultures truly welcome older talent.

We'll return to these organisational dynamics in Chapter 8, where we explore systemic ageism, inclusive practices, and how career professionals can support change from both sides of the table.

45

> **COACHING TOOL 3.2: Skills mapping: Seeing transferable strengths**
>
> This practical exercise helps clients reflect on how their past experiences, paid or unpaid, can translate into future opportunities. It's especially useful for clients with non-linear careers, career breaks, or roles outside formal employment.
>
> Ask your client to complete the table below, exploring not just what they did, but what they enjoyed and how others saw them:
>
> | Role/life phase | Key skills used | Enjoyed/energised by | Strengths others noticed | Applies to... |
> |---|---|---|---|---|
> | Project Manager | Stakeholder engagement, planning | Cross-functional teamwork | Clarity, calm under pressure | Consultancy, operations, event leadership |
> | Community Volunteer | Communication, empathy | Helping others, team spirit | Warmth, reliability | Coaching, HR, community outreach |
> | Team Leader (Retail) | Staff training, conflict resolution | Supporting staff, fast-paced work | Leadership, patience | Learning and development, customer strategy |
> | Caregiving for partner | Scheduling, advocacy, resilience | Making a difference daily | Empathy, problem-solving | Health services, social care, wellbeing |
>
> This type of mapping helps shift clients from deficit thinking 'I've been out of the workforce' to a more empowered narrative: 'I've built capability in different ways.'
>
> **A printable version of this exercise is available in the resources toolkit online. To access, scan the QR code or visit the web address at the start of this book.**

From role to capability

Job titles often limit how clients describe themselves. A title like 'Operations Manager' or 'Project Officer' says little about what the person actually delivered.

The goal is to go beyond generic role descriptions to highlight real capabilities and contributions. Support clients to rephrase experiences with clarity and confidence.

Examples:

- 'I managed a team' to 'I developed others, built culture, and led through uncertainty.'
- 'I organised training sessions' to 'I designed and delivered learning experiences that improved team performance.'
- 'I supported my elderly parents' to 'I coordinated care, managed finances, and advocated across health and social systems.'

Coaching prompts: Translating skills and experience

These prompts help clients uncover the depth behind their roles and reframe experiences in meaningful, transferable ways. Use them to surface strengths, patterns, and future possibilities.

- What skills did you use or develop in each role or life chapter?
- What did you most enjoy, feel proud of, or find energising?
- What strengths or qualities did others consistently notice in you?
- What patterns or themes do you notice across your experiences?
- How might these connect to what you want to do next?

Bridging the language gap

Part of reviewing and rewording experience is learning to speak the language of the next opportunity. Clients may need help moving from internal jargon to sector-relevant terms, or from overly specialist detail to accessible descriptions.

Review a job description together and identify where the client's skills align, even if the wording is different.

Sometimes it's not that a client lacks skills, it's that they don't know how to name and claim them. A client might say, 'I'm not technical', yet they've overseen digital systems, managed data flows, or led tech-integrated projects. Reframing these increases clarity and confidence.

Don't overlook the 'unpaid CV'

Many clients in midlife have done significant work outside formal employment, raising children, caregiving, running community projects, supporting a partner's business, or volunteering. These roles often involve leadership, organisation, creativity, and resilience, yet clients may dismiss them as irrelevant.

Coaches can help surface this invisible labour and reframe it as evidence of capability.

For example, one client who had casually supported a friend's small business with marketing now recognises that contribution, and is using it to build a freelance portfolio.

Helping clients translate their full skill set allows them to show up with greater self-worth. It's not just about making them 'marketable', it's about helping them see themselves differently.

> **MAYA, 56: OWNING THE UNPAID CV**
>
> When Maya first came to coaching, she described herself as 'just helping out', raising children, managing family logistics, and supporting a friend's start-up with marketing. 'None of it counts', she said. 'I've been out of the game for too long.'
>
> Together, we unpacked her experiences: designing flyers, managing social media, coordinating school events. She had a solid track record of project coordination and creative problem-solving.
>
> Her brand words became organised, collaborative, and resourceful. Maya began to see her skills applied beyond home life. 'I haven't been out of the game', she later said. 'I've just been playing it somewhere else.' She now presents herself as a freelance marketing coordinator and is gradually building a portfolio of paid work.
>
> **Coaching reflection:** Many clients, especially women, minimise unpaid or informal work. Coaching can validate lived experience, surface hidden skills, and help clients reframe their story with confidence. Skills gained outside traditional roles are real, transferable, and worth naming.

Networking with purpose

Networking is often one of the most dreaded parts of reinvention, especially for midlife clients who haven't had to do it for years, or who associate it with superficial self-promotion. Many arrive in coaching saying, *'I'm terrible at networking'*, or *'I hate selling myself'*. But when reframed and approached with intention, networking becomes something much more meaningful: a way to build connection, seek insight, and generate new opportunities through authentic relationships.

As coaches, we can help clients shift their mindset from 'networking = selling' to 'networking = learning + sharing'.

The power of warm connections

Clients often believe networking means reaching out to strangers, but many already have a rich network. Old colleagues, past managers, people they volunteered with, clients they supported years ago, these are warm connections that can be reawakened.

Coaching can help clients:

- revisit their network with fresh eyes;
- identify who they'd genuinely like to reconnect with; and
- clarify what they want to explore, ask, or offer.

This isn't about asking for jobs. It's about building visibility and curiosity.

> **Coaching prompt: Reconnecting with warm contacts**
>
> 'Who has seen you at your best?' or 'Who might be happy to hear from you again?'
>
> *This prompt encourages clients to rediscover existing relationships that may hold insight, encouragement, or opportunity, shifting networking from a chore into a meaningful reconnection.*

Strategic, not scattergun

Networking is more effective, and more enjoyable, when it has a clear purpose. Help clients get specific and ask questions such as:

- What do you want to learn?
- Who works in the space you're exploring?
- What kinds of conversations would energise or inform you?

Some clients benefit from crafting a short exploratory message or email they can use to reach out with confidence.

Example outreach message:

Hi [Name], I've been thinking a lot about what's next for me professionally and remembered how much I valued working with you on [project]. I'd love to catch up and hear what you're doing these days. Would you be open to a quick coffee or call in the next few weeks?

Rebuilding confidence through connection

Clients who've stepped away from the workforce, whether for caregiving, redundancy, or personal reasons, often feel their network has gone cold. Reassurance matters here: relationships can be rekindled, especially when outreach is thoughtful and rooted in shared history.

Small wins, like one good conversation, can create momentum and rebuild belief.

As coaches we can suggest:

- reconnecting with two to three people per week;
- starting with peers rather than decision-makers; and
- sharing an article, update, or insight on LinkedIn to warm their visibility.

> **Coaching tip:**
>
> Many clients feel more confident networking when they have a few talking points, recent reflections, a course they've taken, or areas they're exploring. Encourage them to create a list of topics to discuss.

From visibility to possibility

Networking is not just about getting a job; it's about staying visible and engaged in a world of work that is focused on those who are seen. By encouraging clients to focus on relationships, not transactions, we help them access new ideas, build confidence, and generate opportunities that may not even exist yet.

ANGELA, 56: RECONNECTING LEADS TO REINVENTION

After caring for her partner, Angela had been out of the workforce for several years. She didn't know where to begin. In coaching, she mapped her old network. She reached out to a former colleague, just to catch up. That conversation led to a short-term project, which grew into part-time consulting work. Angela's skills hadn't vanished; they'd simply gone unused. Connection reactivated them.

Coaching reflection: Reaching out with curiosity, not pressure, can create new opportunities and remind clients of their worth.

DAVID, 61: VISIBILITY SPARKS OPPORTUNITY

David had been sceptical about social media. 'I'm not one of those people who posts their every thought', he said. But in coaching, he explored how visibility could be about offering value, not self-promotion. He updated his LinkedIn profile with honesty and posted a short reflection on what he'd learned through mentoring. Within a week, a former colleague reached out with a project. That conversation led to a consultancy offer.

Coaching reflection: Thoughtful visibility can shift perception and reopen dormant networks. Sharing your voice invites connection.

Chapter 3: Coaching for Career Reinvention in Midlife

Coaching guide: Supporting clients returning to work in later life

Many clients in their 50s, 60s, or 70s consider returning to work, whether for financial need, purpose, stimulation, or structure. But they often face internal doubts and external barriers. Use these coaching strategies to guide meaningful, realistic work transitions.

1. Clarify the 'why'

Help clients explore their motivation. Is it financial, social, identity-based, or purpose-driven?

Prompt: 'What's drawing you back to work right now, and what would make it worthwhile?'

2. Expand the 'what'

Clients may default to what they've done before. Encourage them to explore adjacent roles, new interests, or flexible pathways like short-term projects or apprenticeships.

Prompt: 'If you could try something just for a season or a year, what would it be?'

3. Inventory skills, including the hidden ones

Support clients in identifying both formal and informal skills, especially those gained through volunteering, caregiving, or community roles.

Prompt: 'What do others come to you for help with?'

Prompt: 'What have you organised, solved, built, or improved, even outside paid work?'

4. Build confidence and counter self-doubt

Age-related confidence dips are common. Challenge internalised ageism with strength-based reflections.

Prompt: 'What life experience gives you an edge others might not have?'

Prompt: 'What part of your story are you not giving enough credit?'

5. Refresh the CV and the story behind it

Work with clients to update how they present themselves on paper and online. Focus on relevance, recent growth, and alignment with the role.

Prompt: 'What would a future employer need to know about who you are now?'

6. Support visibility without performance

Not all clients are comfortable with self-promotion. Explore ways to be visible that feel authentic: mentoring, storytelling, showing up.

Prompt: 'How can you be visible without being loud?'

Prompt: 'Where might your quiet strengths speak for themselves?'

A printable version of this exercise is available in the resources toolkit online. To access, scan the QR code or visit the web address at the start of this book.

Digital presence and visibility

For midlife clients, building a digital presence can feel unfamiliar, uncomfortable, or even unnecessary. Many built successful careers without needing to 'market' themselves online. But in today's world, digital visibility is more than a nice-to-have, it's a signal of relevance, confidence, and professional currency.

A strong online presence helps clients:

- reinforce their personal brand;
- be discoverable by recruiters, collaborators, or former colleagues;
- share their thinking and values in a way that builds trust.

As coaches, we can help clients approach this with authenticity and intention, not pressure or perfectionism.

Why LinkedIn matters

LinkedIn is the default professional platform. Even clients who aren't actively job seeking are likely to be looked up online by others, potential employers, collaborators, or former contacts. A neglected profile can unintentionally send the message: *I'm not current* or *I'm not active*.

A well-crafted LinkedIn profile, on the other hand, can:

- show who they are becoming, not just who they've been;
- communicate credibility and energy;
- act as a conversation starter for networking or consulting opportunities.

Doug, 61, landed a consulting role after updating his LinkedIn profile and sharing a personal reflection post.

Coaching clients to optimise their profile

Here are some key areas to focus on in coaching conversations:

1. Headline

Encourage clients to go beyond their last job title. Use this space to reflect the type of work they're moving toward. There are 220 characters available and this can be a positioning statement or a series of key words

For someone moving into portfolio or flexible consultancy work:
Former HR Director | Now Supporting Teams through Change, Conflict and Culture Work | Available for Projects and Mentoring

- This emphasises transferable expertise while making space for the new direction.

For someone pivoting towards purpose-led part-time or community work:
Experienced Administrator | Passionate about Local Impact, People Support and Practical Solutions | Open to Flexible Roles

- This keeps it warm, capable, and values-led, ideal for clients moving into non-profit, part-time, or community-based roles.

For someone moving into creativity or learning roles:
Former Teacher | Now Designing Creative Workshops for Lifelong Learners | Interested in Arts, Learning, and Community Engagement

- This communicates a clear past–present narrative and aligns with values around creativity and contribution without sounding inflated.

2. About/summary section

This is where the personal brand story comes to life. Guide clients to write in the first person, highlight key strengths, and express values or vision. It's a chance to tell your story.

> **Coaching prompt: Defining your digital signature**
>
> 'What do you want to be known for?'
>
> *This prompt helps clients clarify their personal brand and articulate a core message that can shape their LinkedIn profile and online presence.*

3. Featured section

Encourage clients to add a post, article, project, or link, something that illustrates their thinking or recent work.

4. Banner image

This is a visual opportunity to reinforce their personal brand, whether it's a calm workspace, thematic image, or relevant quote.

5. Activity

Clients don't have to post constantly, but engaging with posts, commenting, or sharing insights a few times a month builds presence.

Working with digital discomfort

Some clients worry about being judged, rejected, or appearing boastful. These feelings often stem from deeper fears around visibility and self-worth. As coaches, we can hold space for those fears while encouraging small, low-risk steps forward.

Ideas include:

- commenting on someone else's post;
- reposting an article with a one-sentence takeaway;
- sharing a story about what they've learned in their career.

These micro-actions build confidence and connection, without the pressure of full-scale self-promotion.

Coaching prompt: Sharing with authenticity

'What's one thing you could share that reflects who you are, not just what you've done?'

This prompt helps clients overcome digital discomfort by focusing on small, values-based actions that build confidence and connection online.

Beyond LinkedIn: Personal websites or portfolios

For clients moving into consulting, creative, or portfolio work, a simple personal website can be a helpful extension of their brand. It doesn't have to be elaborate, just a clean, professional space to outline services, share a bio, and offer a way to get in touch.

Some clients may also use tools like:

- Medium or Substack (for sharing thought leadership);
- Canva portfolios (for visual work or project summaries); and
- Linktree (for service overviews or resource hubs).

The key is to meet clients where they are and support them to take the next visible step, however small.

Sample LinkedIn summary (for a midlife reinvention story)
About

After 25 years leading teams in the corporate world, I've transitioned into freelance consultancy focused on helping mission-led organisations thrive.

My career has always centred around building systems, people, and momentum, from operations and project management to leadership development.

I bring calm under pressure, clarity in complexity, and a deep belief in values-based work.

Now, I work with organisations navigating change, helping them realign strategy, simplify operations, and support their people.

I'm especially interested in part-time, project-based, or advisory work that allows space for creativity, flexibility, and impact.

Let's connect.

Invite clients to write a 'first draft' that prioritises voice over polish, what matters most is clarity and energy, not perfection.

Positioning for flexible work and phased retirement

Stepping up, down, or across: Career moves in midlife and beyond

Not every career move is about climbing higher. In midlife and later-life, the direction of travel may shift, and that's not a failure. It's a recalibration.

Some people step up, using their experience to take on more senior or purpose-driven roles. Others choose to step down, reclaiming time and energy for other areas of life. And some step across, into different sectors, interim roles, or contract work that offers greater autonomy or alignment.

Interim and bridging roles can be especially valuable. They create breathing space, reduce pressure, and allow experimentation. Whether it's a short-term contract, a part-time opportunity, or a consultancy trial, these moves can act as stepping stones into your next chapter, without the weight of permanence.

The important thing is not the label, but the fit. Ask your client: what direction supports who you are now, and what matters most?

For many midlife clients, especially those in their late 50s or 60s, the goal is no longer to climb but to shape work that fits the life they want to lead. Some seek flexibility to manage caregiving or health. Others want to reduce intensity without losing impact. Still others want to step into work that feels more aligned, meaningful, or energising.

What they often need help with is *positioning*: how to present themselves to the market in a way that reflects both competence and availability, without signalling decline, disengagement, or irrelevance.

Coaching towards the work–life blend

Clients may be exploring different types of work: part-time or project-based work; portfolio or freelance careers; interim or consulting roles; 'Bridge jobs' that allow gradual winding down and perhaps retiring from full-time roles but not from purpose.

> **Coaching prompts: Positioning for flexible work and phased retirement**
>
> *These prompts support clients in clarifying what kind of work they want, how it fits their life stage, and how to communicate that clearly and confidently.*
>
> - What type of work do you want, and why?
> - What kind of structure supports your energy and lifestyle now?
> - How do you want to communicate your availability and value to others?
> - What role do you want work to play in your life now?

Language matters

Clients often worry that asking for flexibility will undermine their credibility. They fear being seen as less ambitious, less capable, or *winding down*. Part of coaching is helping them own what they want without apology.

Here are three ways clients might confidently frame flexibility:

- 'I'm currently focusing on project-based or interim roles where I can add value quickly.'
- 'I'm seeking part-time work in a mission-led organisation where I can contribute my experience while maintaining flexibility.'
- 'I've moved into a portfolio career: consulting, mentoring, and taking on short-term contracts in [field].'

This kind of language is clear, confident, and forward-looking. It doesn't dwell on limitations; it focuses on fit.

Building a flexible identity

Sometimes clients need help adjusting their own self-concept. If they've been in traditional, full-time employment for decades, stepping into a more fluid work identity can feel unfamiliar.

Coaches can encourage experimentation:

- take on one small freelance project to test the waters;
- join a non-exec board or advisory group;
- offer mentoring or training on a flexible basis.

These experiences can help build confidence and credibility in new ways of working, and open unexpected doors.

Preparing for mixed messaging

It's also worth preparing clients for mixed responses. Some recruiters or employers still cling to traditional models. Not every workplace is ready for phased retirement, portfolio careers, or flexible working in later-life. Clients need to be ready to advocate for themselves, without being discouraged by resistance.

That's where a strong narrative helps. When clients can explain *why* they're choosing this path and *how* it connects to their values and strengths, they become much more compelling.

MALCOLM, 60: REDEFINING AMBITION, CHOOSING IMPACT OVER HOURS

Malcolm had worked in engineering for decades. He didn't want to stop working, but full-time roles no longer appealed. Through coaching, he recognised that his sense of ambition had changed. It wasn't about building status, it was about mentoring others, using his experience in smaller, purposeful ways. He now consults part-time and supports apprentices. 'I'm still ambitious', he said. 'Just in a different direction.'

Coaching reflection: Ambition doesn't disappear, it evolves. Clients often need help giving voice to this new version of success.

NADIA, 56: SHAPING A PORTFOLIO CAREER WITH PURPOSE

Nadia had worked in education leadership but longed for more flexibility and variety. She left her full-time role and began shaping a portfolio career, combining teaching, coaching, and community work. Some friends questioned the decision. 'Why give up a stable job?' But Nadia knew she was building something that aligned with her values and energy. In coaching, she developed her narrative and became confident explaining her path. She now calls herself 'a purposeful pluralist'.

Coaching reflection: Portfolio careers require coherence in messaging. Support clients in integrating their strands into a compelling whole.

Bridging towards retirement, not jumping off a cliff

For some clients, flexible work is a bridge towards retirement. For others, it's simply a smarter way to work. Either way, coaches can support them to think holistically, not just about income or hours, but about meaning, energy, and contribution.

Evergreen strategy

As people begin to consider longer lives, potentially into their 90s or beyond, *(ONS 2023: 1 in 6 girls born today are expected to live to 100)* career coaching must evolve to reflect this reality. Economist Andrew Scott describes the need for an 'evergreening strategy': a proactive investment in health, learning, purpose, and social capital to sustain vitality and adaptability over extended lifespans.

For clients in midlife, this mindset shift is essential. It supports not just longer careers, but more flexible, creative, and fulfilling ones. Encouraging investment in lifelong learning, energy, and relationships becomes not just personal growth but strategic career planning.

Helping clients imagine a phased working life, one shaped by purpose-led pivots, part-time reinvention, or evolving contribution, aligns powerfully with this evergreening approach. Coaching prompts such as 'What might a work–life rhythm look like in your 70s?' or 'Which of your skills do you want to carry forward, and which to let go?' help bridge the gap between traditional career planning and modern later-life design.

COACHING TOOL 3.3: Designing your ideal week

This reflective exercise helps clients imagine a realistic and fulfilling rhythm of life two to three years from now. It supports clarity around future priorities and helps align work identity with personal values.

Instructions:

Invite your client to sketch their *ideal week* – not a fantasy escape, but a balanced, meaningful life chapter. Ask them to consider:

- What activities fill each day?
- What is the balance between work, leisure, learning, and connection?
- How much structure or freedom do they want?
- What kind of energy do they want to feel?

This future vision becomes a foundation for career planning, helping clients shape roles, opportunities, or work identities that support the life they want to lead.

Optional prompt:

Once the week is sketched, ask:
'What would need to change for this version of life to become possible?'

When life affects work: Health, caregiving, and relationships

Career reinvention in midlife rarely happens in ideal conditions. Unlike early career shifts, which may be fuelled by ambition or exploration, many midlife transitions are shaped, or constrained, by real-life responsibilities. Health concerns, caregiving demands, and changing family or financial dynamics can significantly influence a client's choices, timing, and capacity.

For coaches, this means staying attuned not just to career aspirations, but to the broader life context in which those aspirations are unfolding.

The impact of health
Some clients arrive in coaching after a serious diagnosis or chronic condition. Others face reduced energy, recurring pain, or mental health challenges. These physical and emotional shifts can reshape what's realistic or desirable.

Coaching questions might include:

- What kind of work supports your health right now?
- What are your energy rhythms, and how can work adapt to them?
- What kinds of environments support your wellbeing?

Helping clients assess not just what they *can* do but what they can do *sustainably* is key.

The caregiving conundrum
Many midlife clients are balancing work with caregiving responsibilities; for ageing parents, ill partners, grandchildren, or even adult children returning home. These roles are often invisible on a CV, but they take real time, energy, and emotional bandwidth.

Clients may:

- step back from career progression;
- seek flexible or part-time roles; and/or
- take career breaks, and then struggle to re-enter.

Coaches can validate the emotional complexity here, while also helping clients recognise the skills and strengths caregiving builds: planning, negotiation, empathy, resilience, and advocacy.

Coaching prompts: Reflecting on the impact of caregiving

Explore how caregiving has shaped the client's values, work preferences, and sense of purpose.

You might ask:

- What strengths have you developed through caregiving?
- How has this experience changed what matters to you in work and life?
- In what ways has caregiving influenced the kind of role, environment, or schedule you want now?

These prompts help clients name and value the transferable skills and personal growth caregiving brings, often hidden from traditional career conversations.

Relationship shifts and financial realities

Divorce, bereavement, or a partner's career change can also affect reinvention. Some clients are re-entering the workforce after years out of the paid labour market. Others find themselves needing income quickly due to separation, loss, or unexpected financial shocks.

This may lead to tension between what clients want and what they feel they can afford to pursue. Coaches can help clients explore short-term stability steps alongside longer-term aspirations, keeping hope alive without denying reality.

JULIE, 55: REBUILDING ON HER TERMS – FINDING STABILITY AFTER SETBACK

After her divorce, Julie needed to return to paid work quickly. 'I wanted to do something meaningful', she said, 'but I also needed to pay the bills'. Coaching helped her take a pragmatic role as a university administrator: steady hours, decent income, close to home. It wasn't her dream job, but it gave her structure and breathing space.

Over time, she completed a part-time coaching course, built a network through volunteering, and eventually launched her own small practice supporting women in transition. 'Taking that admin job felt like a step backwards', she reflected, 'but it gave me the foundation to rebuild on my terms'.

Coaching reflection: Stability can be a stepping stone. Coaching helps clients reframe pragmatic choices as foundations for future growth and self-directed change.

TOM, 60: SLOWER STEPS, DEEPER MEANING

Tom lost his wife unexpectedly and, with it, much of the financial stability they had planned for retirement. Grieving and unsure what to do next, he knew he needed income but couldn't face returning to his previous high-pressure role in finance. 'I didn't have the energy for that version of me anymore', he said. Through coaching, Tom identified a bridge job in a local housing association, less pay, but manageable hours and a mission that felt meaningful. It gave him a place to show up each day, gently rebuild confidence, and process what mattered most. A year later, he began mentoring younger colleagues and exploring part-time financial coaching for community groups. 'This isn't the path I imagined', he said, 'but it's one I've grown into'.

Coaching reflection: After loss, clients may need slower steps and gentler goals. Coaching supports meaningful re-entry that honours both grief and emerging purpose.

Holding the whole story

Clients don't just bring their CV to coaching, they bring their whole lives. Effective midlife career coaching means holding space for grief, fatigue, joy, ambition, and everything in between.

Sometimes the most powerful thing a coach can do is say, *'It makes sense that this feels hard.'* From that place of validation, we can co-create strategies that honour both the person and their reality.

Coaching prompts: Holding the whole story

These prompts helps clients consider not just what they want to do next, but how to move forward in a way that honours their energy, experiences, and inner life.

You might ask:

- What do you need to protect, preserve, or prioritise in this next chapter?
- What parts of your life or self feels most important to carry forward right now?
- What boundaries or supports might you need to protect what matters most?
- What's asking for attention, even if it doesn't fit neatly on a CV?

The coach's role in reinvention

Midlife reinvention is both a professional and psychological journey. While clients may come to coaching seeking help with CVs, job search strategies, or interview preparation, what they often need most is a space to be seen, heard, and supported as they navigate deep questions of identity, purpose, and possibility.

The coach's role is to hold this space with clarity, compassion, and challenge, blending career strategy with emotional insight.

From technician to thinking partner

Midlife clients often arrive with complex stories. Their careers have chapters, layers, and meaning. They don't need a technician; they need a thinking partner. Someone who can help them make sense of where they've been and envision where they might go next.

As coaches, we're not just supporting a job move; we're supporting a life move.

That may involve:

- gently surfacing internalised narratives about age, value, or visibility;
- helping clients reclaim their voice and agency;
- encouraging experimentation and prototyping over perfectionism; and
- normalising non-linear paths and layered identities.

Supporting courage and momentum

Reinvention requires courage. Clients may fear rejection, visibility, irrelevance, or failure. They may have moments of self-doubt, ambivalence, or overwhelm. The coach's role is not to rush them, but to walk alongside them, holding belief until they can hold it for themselves.

Coaches can help clients to reframe setbacks as feedback, recognise and name their evolving strengths, encourage them to share their story with confidence and clarity and to support them to take one meaningful step at a time.

Coaching prompts: Supporting courage and momentum

Reinvention takes emotional energy. Scaling questions can help track shifts in confidence and clarify what support is needed next.

Try asking:

- 'On a scale of 1–10, how confident do you feel about this direction?'
- 'What would help move you one point higher?'
- 'What's one small step you could take that feels doable right now?'

These prompts help clients monitor their progress, build momentum, and stay connected to their inner resources, even when the path feels uncertain.

Balancing vision with practicality

Midlife clients need to dream; but they also need structure. Vision without action creates anxiety. Action without vision leads to restlessness. Coaches can offer both: permission to dream and tools to move forward.

This might mean helping clients with practical activities such as to draft a compelling LinkedIn summary, map their transferable skills, develop a networking plan that feels doable, and practise telling a career story that reflects who they are now.

Reinvention as redefinition, not repair

Reinvention is not about fixing something broken. It's about becoming more congruent with who they are now. The coach's role is to reflect that evolving identity, sometimes before the client can see it for themselves.

As coaches we can reflect on what new identity is trying to emerge in our client, and how can we help them articulate it, try it on, and grow into it?

Closing reflections

I've worked with hundreds of clients in midlife, and reinvention is rarely about starting over. It's about returning to what matters. It's about recognising what no longer fits and daring to imagine what might.

At this stage of life, coaching becomes something deeper than career guidance. We're helping people reorient, to listen inward, reframe long-held narratives, and take ownership of a future that feels more honest and alive. Every client brings with them a lifetime of insight. Our role is to help them name it, claim it, and shape it into something that fits who they are now.

For me, this work continues to be meaningful because I've gone through some of these transitions myself. And each time I witness someone take even a small, courageous step toward reinvention, it reminds me how much possibility still lives in this phase of life.

 In a nutshell

- Reinvention is often more about alignment and identity than dramatic change.
- Clients can use small experiments (prototyping) to explore new directions with less pressure.
- Strategic positioning and personal branding play a role in shifting from job title to value-led identity.
- Practical tools can help translate skills, map strengths, and tell a coherent career story.
- Confidence and authenticity are key when approaching networking, digital visibility, and flexible work.
- Holding space for life context – such as health, caregiving, and loss – and helping clients honour ambition and reality are important.

Chapter 4
The psychology of retirement and identity shifts

Summary

Retirement is more than a career transition: it's a profound shift in identity, meaning, and daily rhythm. This chapter explores the psychological dimensions of retirement, including loss, freedom, generativity, and the search for purpose. It offers coaches tools to support clients through uncertainty, help them reframe identity, and create lives beyond work that feel meaningful, aligned, and alive.

Retirement as an identity transition

Retirement is not just a career change; it's a fundamental shift in how we see ourselves. While it can be a time of liberation and new possibilities, many clients experience uncertainty, loss, or a sense of invisibility. This chapter explores the psychological landscape of retirement and how coaches can support clients through identity shifts, purpose exploration, and the redefinition of self in later life.

When I ran pre-retirement seminars, I often noticed how few people wanted to think about identity or purpose. Their focus was typically on holidays, grandchildren, or home improvements. And yet, two years later, some would get back in touch, feeling adrift and asking, 'Is this it?' That's why we, as coaches, must raise these deeper questions early, but not always expect clients to be ready to discuss. Through my academic research, I found there is often a one- to two-year transitional period after leaving full-time work, a liminal phase where people are adjusting. We must honour this timing, gently supporting reflection without rushing it.

>
> **Reflective practice: Reflecting on shifting identity**
>
> How confident are you in raising identity and meaning before clients articulate distress? How might you introduce these gently and early?

Understanding the retirement transition

Clients will come to you at different points in their journey:

- Those just beginning to plan for retirement.
- Those already retired but experiencing restlessness or loss.
- Those returning after a break, considering new options.

Many imagine retirement as an extended holiday, and in the beginning, it often is. A big trip, some decorating, days out, time with family, and a more leisurely pace of life all contribute to a satisfying first phase. For some, this continues. But others find the novelty wears off. Those are the people who may contact you when the excitement fades and deeper questions about meaning emerge.

As career coaches, we often meet clients navigating complex emotions, shifting identities, and uncertain futures. While retirement can bring freedom and joy, it can also provoke feelings of confusion, loss, and vulnerability.

This chapter blends practical coaching guidance with a deeper psychological understanding. Most coach training doesn't include retirement theory, so my aim here is to equip you with insights that go beyond what your clients may have encountered.

The historical perspective

Retirement today is a far cry from what our parents and grandparents experienced. In earlier generations, people often had physically demanding lives: men in manual jobs, women running households without labour-saving technology. By retirement age, rest was not just earned but needed.

Today, we live longer and hope to remain in reasonable health into our mid-70s and beyond. Retirement now happens in a vastly more diverse social and economic context. For some, it begins comfortably at 60, with a focus on leisure and unpaid activities. Others are still struggling to earn an income after redundancy, with pensions years away. Health, too, is no longer a constant; we coach people with widely varying physical and cognitive capacities.

You may be asked to deliver a preparation-for-retirement course or work one-to-one with people seeking guidance. Either way, you'll encounter a wide spectrum of expectations, emotions, and realities.

As we enter our 60s, retirement can mean many things. For some, it's a distinct phase of life marked by the clean break from work and a transition into leisure. Others continue working, either because they want to or because they need to, often in reduced or more flexible roles. They might pursue encore careers, take on purpose-driven jobs, or volunteer. Increasingly, people want to remain mentally and physically active.

A Merrill Lynch and Age Wave survey found that over 60% of retirees wanted to continue working to stay mentally active, and 46% to remain physically active.

Some people stop seeing retirement as a defined life phase at all. This is where I see the future heading. Many will move in and out of paid work, caregiving, study, volunteering, and sabbaticals. They may follow this pattern until they reach 'old-old' age and can no longer continue. This non-linear life model breaks down the traditional work–retirement binary and offers a broader canvas for coaching conversations.

Where is your client on their retirement journey? Anticipating, adjusting, or redefining their path?

When retirement isn't a choice

Retirement isn't always voluntary. Some clients are nudged, or pushed, into it.

Barry noticed subtle shifts at work. Younger colleagues started saying things like, 'Aren't you ready to slow down?' And others his age were quietly leaving. He began to wonder if it was time for him too.

Lyn, in her early 60s, felt she had no option but to stop working. She became a full-time carer for both her mother and husband.

Margaret, on the other hand, was burned out after years in a demanding role. Thanks to a final salary pension, she had the option to retire early and chose to focus on long-postponed interests.

Not everyone reaches this transition on equal footing. As coaches, we must be sensitive to whether retirement is chosen, forced, or reluctantly accepted.

One of the first areas to cover with our clients is about how they come to be discussing retirement. Is this down to personal choice like Margaret, or something they have accepted? This can shape their outlook and underpin how they are feeling as they begin their coaching with you.

Beyond paid work: The value of unpaid contribution

Reaching state pension age should not mark the end of our contribution to society. While governments may want older adults to stay in the workforce for economic reasons, many people remain active contributors through unpaid work. They volunteer, mentor, support communities, and care for family members. This is essential work, just not financially compensated.

The concept of *productive ageing* has evolved to include these unpaid forms of contribution. It matters not only for society but for the individual's sense of purpose, belonging, and worth.

Many people only begin to reflect on this once the initial excitement of retirement fades. That's why raising these questions early, before they feel adrift, can make such a meaningful difference in their transition.

Reflective practice: Reflecting on shifting identity

How can you help clients value unpaid contributions as a vital expression of identity and purpose?

Identity, purpose, and the changing self

As a client considers their options; we need to get them to think of what will be right for them, as they are now. Questions that we can ask include:

- To what extent is identity important to you?
- What gives you meaning and a sense of accomplishment?
- How will you live in line with your values?
- What will give you space to develop and grow?

Let's start by guiding our clients to review their working life and how satisfied they were with it.

Work
Some people love their job and can't imagine life without it. They may have few other interests or hobbies; they live and breathe work. For these

individuals, stopping work can be incredibly difficult. Some never do. They continue in their job with little thought to what else might be possible, only realising, often too late, that they've missed out on other dimensions of life.

Others stay in work because it provides an emotional high. For those who are effectively addicted to work, completing tasks, responding to emails, producing reports, or receiving praise releases neurotransmitters like serotonin and dopamine. These create short-term feelings of happiness and pride, rewarding them for being busy. When not working, they may even feel a withdrawal from that emotional feedback loop.

Who are we without the title?

For many people, the deepest challenge in retirement is not the lack of structure or routine, it is the loss of identity. One retired client confided, 'If I'm not a doctor anymore, who am I?' This is not uncommon, especially among individuals whose work roles were tightly woven into their sense of self.

Philosopher Marianne Janack writes that retirement is not just a financial decision; it is a profoundly existential one. Drawing on thinkers like Kant and Sartre, she explores the idea that we become what we do. When we've spent decades performing, producing, and being useful, often judged by our output, it is no surprise that retirement may feel like a kind of disappearance.

Kant warned against reducing people to tools, objects valued only for their utility. Yet in modern work culture, many professionals have come to view themselves exactly that way, measured by contribution, productivity, or title. Retirement disrupts this framing, but doesn't automatically offer a new one. It's a transition that asks: If I am no longer useful in the way I was, do I still matter?

Helping clients untangle their identity from their job title is some of the most important work a career coach can do in later life. The goal is not to dismiss the past role, but to expand the definition of self: to shift from 'I was' to 'I am becoming'.

> **Coaching prompts: Identity beyond role or title**
>
> *These prompts support clients in exploring how identity shifts after leaving a long-held role. They help surface values, strengths, and emerging self-concepts, beyond titles, productivity, or external validation.*
>
> - When you introduce yourself now, how do you describe who you are?
> - What words feel most natural, and which feel awkward or unfamiliar?
> - How much of your self-worth was tied to your job title or professional role?
> - What parts of your identity still hold true, even without that title?
> - What aspects of your work role reflected deeper values or strengths you still carry? Are there ways to express those qualities differently now?
> - What do you fear others see, or don't see, when/if you say you're retired?
> - How would you like to reshape that narrative, for yourself or others?
> - Who are you becoming now? What would it look like to define yourself by what you're drawn to, rather than what you produce?

Loss of status

One of the more hidden but powerful elements in the transition to retirement is the loss of status. While clients may speak of missing routine, challenge, or connection, often beneath these is a subtler grief: not being seen in the same way.

'We need to reimagine ageing as a process of opening up rather than shutting down.' – Carl Honoré

In coaching, this matters. Many clients struggle not with retirement itself, but with the sudden absence of recognition. A former CEO becomes a 'former', still the same person, but perceived differently. A teacher or manager loses the subtle esteem that comes from role and routine. They may say, 'I feel invisible' or 'I'm not sure who I am now', and we can help name what's beneath that: the loss of status.

Honoré suggests five ways to navigate this shift: talking honestly about status, embracing new forms of esteem rooted in purpose and service, diversifying the places we gain validation, lifting our gaze to broader meaning, and seeking connection in smaller, authentic communities. He reminds us that true fulfilment often comes not from widespread acclaim but from being known, not by many, but by a few who truly see us.

Adapted from Carl Honoré, 'From CEO to TBD: Status and the Midlife Reset' (2024).

Chapter 4: The Psychology of Retirement and Identity Shifts

Coaching prompts: Navigating the loss of status

These prompts support clients in uncovering the emotional layers beneath retirement transitions, particularly the subtle loss of recognition and role-based esteem.

You might ask:

- Where did you feel most valued in your working life, and by whom?
- What kinds of recognition do you miss, and what might replace or reframe them now?
- What would it mean to redefine status on your own terms in this next chapter?

These prompts help clients name hidden losses and begin to imagine more self-defined, purpose-driven forms of esteem.

For some, work is simply a means to an end. **Simon,** for example, couldn't wait to retire. He had a few plans, but they didn't quite work out, and he drifted for several years before reconnecting with himself.

Many of my clients have been excited to move into something new. Some chose new jobs where money was no longer the driver, they had an occupational pension, so they could finally do what they loved. Others, like **Henry,** focused more on voluntary activities and interests that brought satisfaction.

Linda said 'I thought I'd want part-time consultancy after retiring. But after a year, I realised what I needed wasn't more work, it was space to become someone new. I just didn't know how to begin.'

And me? At 61, I chose a different kind of investment, starting a doctorate and training as a Wilderness Rites of Passage guide. It wasn't about earning more, but about growing, learning, and listening more deeply to life.

Coaching prompts: Reimagining growth

- What does growth mean to you now – not professionally but personally or spiritually?
- Where might you stretch, deepen, or rediscover yourself next?

Whether clients are looking for paid work, voluntary roles, or a new and absorbing hobby, it helps to start by reviewing their career history and reflecting on what work has meant to them.

For many, work provides not only income but also structure, identity, and meaning. As retirement approaches, this can leave clients disoriented. They may cling to their job title or feel uncertain and diminished without it.

The question many clients ask is: Who am I now? Who am I without my work? What gives my life meaning today?

Carl Jung viewed the second half of life as a time to turn inward, a shift from outward striving to inner reflection. He wrote of the need to move from looking outwards to looking into oneself, a process he saw as essential to becoming whole.

He believed that this later-life phase was about individuation, becoming more whole. It's no longer about productivity in the traditional sense, but about self-understanding, alignment with deeper values, and becoming who we were meant to be.

> **COACHING TOOL 4.1: Rituals for closure**
>
> In grief traditions, rituals like storytelling, silent presence, or symbolic acts (e.g. tearing a garment or walking with others) help people process endings and honour what was lost. Clients navigating the end of a work identity may benefit from adapted rituals that allow for reflection, dignity, and psychological closure.
>
> *Coaching exercise: Create your own closure ritual*
>
> Invite your client to develop a small, meaningful ritual that acknowledges their work life:
>
> - Writing a letter to the role or organisation they're leaving.
> - Taking a photo of their workspace or team as a keepsake.
> - Gathering stories or 'career highlights' from colleagues.
> - Sharing one final 'lesson learned' on LinkedIn or in a personal blog.
>
> These symbolic acts can validate the significance of what was lost, and make space for what's next.

Coaching prompts: Identity, purpose, and the changing self

These prompts help clients explore who they are becoming, what matters now, and how identity evolves beyond work. Use them to surface values, legacy, growth, and inner alignment.

You might ask:

- To what extent is identity important to you now?
- What gives you meaning and a sense of accomplishment?
- What have you gained from working, beyond your salary?
- What parts of your identity are you ready to let go of, and what's waiting to grow?
- What roles have defined you, and which ones no longer fit?

To deepen reflection further:

- What will give you space to develop and grow in this next phase?
- How will you live more in line with your values?
- What kind of legacy, if any, do you want to leave?
- If your life were a story, what chapter are you in now, and what do you want the next one to be called?

Exploring status and belonging:

- What does being valued look like for you now?
- What communities, roles, or pursuits still affirm your worth?
- What would it mean to have 'enough' status, and who gets to define that?

Cognition and the retirement transition

Retirement isn't just a lifestyle change; it can be a neurological one too. The sudden loss of routine, stimulation, and social connection can affect how the brain functions. Research from long-term studies, such as the Whitehall II project on retirement and memory, shows that some retirees experience sharper declines in memory, focus, or mood, particularly those leaving cognitively demanding or identity-defining roles.

Clients may describe feeling scattered, foggy, or emotionally flat in the months after stepping away from work. This isn't necessarily cognitive decline; it's often the brain's response to a loss of mental structure.

The good news? The brain is adaptable well into later life. With the right approach, retirement can become a period of growth rather than deterioration.

Purposeful social interaction, learning new skills, and engaging in creative or physical activities all help protect and enhance cognitive health.

As coaches, we can help clients prepare for this shift, not just financially but mentally and emotionally. That means encouraging the development of new routines, exploring non-work identities, and planning ways to stay stimulated and connected after retirement.

What helps?
- Building new routines before leaving work.
- Staying socially engaged, especially through meaningful, in-person interactions.
- Pursuing learning, creativity, and physical activity.
- Volunteering or contributing in ways that feel purposeful.

Staying sharp isn't about crossword puzzles, it's about staying connected to life.

Life stage coaching

Clients in their 50s, 60s, 70s and beyond, often have very different emotional, financial, and identity-related needs, but as coaches, it helps to think developmentally, not just chronologically.

Reappraising and repositioning (typically experienced in the 50s)

Clients are typically still working but beginning to think ahead. They may want to pivot into a different kind of role, reduce hours, or explore legacy, autonomy, and future flexibility. Some are at their peak earning years, yet feel restless or burned out. Others are still actively seeking advancement, with no intention of stepping back, like Sarah from Chapter 1.

Rebalancing and redefining (typically experienced in the 60s)

This is often the most emotionally complex life stage. There may be a desire to retire or reduce hours, alongside feelings of anxiety, guilt, or grief. Some are managing caring responsibilities or recovering from burnout. For others, this is a time of rebirth, starting something new or unexpected. Take Anita, 60, who stepped away from work after caring for her father. She gradually found purpose again through part-time mentoring at a local social enterprise.

Reimagining and reconnecting (typically experienced in the 70s and beyond)

Clients may have exited paid work, but their desire for purpose and engagement remains strong. Many reengage with creative pursuits, learning, volunteering, or spiritual and philosophical reflection. Work identity may have faded, but expression and contribution continue in new forms. Josie, who achieved career success early and had children later, felt more energised at 60 than some of her younger peers. Now in her 70s, she was planning her 'next chapter' around creativity, travel, and deeper connection.

Reflective practice: Coach reflection in practice

What developmental tasks or patterns are surfacing for your client at this stage of life?

Generativity and giving back

You may be familiar with Erikson's eight stages of development, which begin in infancy with trust versus mistrust and move through identity and intimacy. By midlife, the core task becomes generativity: a concern for the wellbeing of future generations and a desire to leave something of value behind. In later life, the focus shifts to ego integrity versus despair, where meaning and reflection take centre stage.

Erikson's psychosocial stage of generativity versus stagnation speaks powerfully to this phase of life. In midlife, which used to be from the early 40s into the 60s, but now seems to have moved on a decade, many clients feel a deep desire to give back: to mentor, volunteer, support younger people, or contribute to causes that matter. They want to feel useful. They want their lives to matter to someone else.

Generativity can be expressed formally or informally. It might involve leadership, mentoring, creating something meaningful, or simply being present for others in a supportive or caring role. It's about contribution, adding value beyond the self.

Generative adults create environments, at home, in communities, or within institutions, where others can grow and thrive. When that generative impulse is blocked or unexpressed, stagnation can creep in. It may show up as boredom, restlessness, or a sense of emotional drift.

In my research, generativity emerged as a strong predictor of both job satisfaction and attitudes towards retirement. Clients who continue to create, care, and contribute tend to feel more purposeful and fulfilled. Those who don't may find themselves asking, 'Is this it?' a question that often signals the early stirrings of something deeper: the human impulse to leave a legacy.

> **COACHING TOOL 4.2: Legacy reflection exercise: What do you want to leave behind?**
>
> This exercise helps clients explore the kind of impact they want to have, not in terms of money or status, but in how they shape the world around them and how they'll be remembered.
>
> ### Step 1: Prompt
>
> Ask your client to complete the following sentence: 'I want to be remembered for . . .'
>
> Encourage them to write freely for 5–10 minutes, without editing or overthinking. Let it be emotional, aspirational, or even surprising.
>
> ### Step 2: Expand
>
> Now invite them to reflect further:
>
> - Whose lives do you hope to influence or touch?
> - What values do you want to pass on?
> - What stories or experiences would you like people to talk about you?
> - What quiet contributions might matter most in the long run?
> - What are you creating, nurturing, or stewarding that might outlast you?
>
> ### Step 3: Bring it closer
>
> Ask: 'What might you do this year that aligns with the legacy you want to leave?'
>
> This grounds the idea of legacy in present-day choices and encourages action in service of long-term meaning.
>
> - 'Where do you feel called to make a difference now?'

Research suggests that generativity is a strong predictor of satisfaction in retirement. It provides a sense of continuity and connection between one's past experience and future impact.

There are many paths towards generativity. It might be:

- volunteering for a cause or organisation that aligns with your values;
- mentoring someone younger, formally or informally;
- supporting a young person transitioning from foster care into independent living;
- sharing your experience in a creative or educational way; or
- deepening relationships with younger people and staying open to their perspectives.

Even casual conversations can open generative doorways. When we listen more deeply and stay curious, we spot opportunities to encourage, support, or guide others. Sometimes, we receive just as much in return, what some call reverse mentoring. Younger people think differently, and their energy and outlook can broaden our own.

HELEN, 73: RECLAIMING IDENTITY THROUGH LOCAL HISTORY

Helen, a former barrister, had always loved history. After retiring, she became a local historian. When introduced, she no longer said, 'I used to be a barrister', she said, 'I'm a historian'. This new identity felt far more alive than 'retired barrister.' If we don't keep generating value or engaging with the world, it's easy to slide into stagnation. But the question 'Is this it?' often signals not an end, but the beginning of a more generative chapter.

Coaching reflection: Help clients name the new identities they are growing into, not just the professional ones they've left behind. Identity in later life is not about what we used to be, but what we choose to become.

Reflective practice: Coach reflection in practice

Where does your client feel most alive, and how can that be nurtured?

Identity beyond job titles

Retirement can provoke a deep identity shift. Without a professional title to fall back on, many clients feel uncertain, invisible, or undervalued. Saying 'I used to be a . . .' or simply 'I'm retired' can feel hollow, especially for those whose sense of self was closely tied to their work.

We are conditioned to answer the question 'What do you do?' with a job title. Once that role disappears, many clients struggle to answer. But we were always more than our jobs. Later life offers an opportunity to reclaim and redefine identity, not around performance or hierarchy but around authenticity and alignment.

This is where coaching becomes invaluable. We can help clients:

- explore who they are without work;
- redefine their identity beyond labels and roles;
- discover new ways of showing up in the world; and
- accept that identity shifts are not a loss, but a step towards wholeness.

Coaching prompt: Identity beyond job titles

'What do you want to be known for in this next stage of life?'

This prompt helps clients move beyond professional labels to consider the qualities, contributions, and presence they want to be remembered or recognised for.

You might also ask:

- What parts of you were overlooked while you were working?
- How would you introduce yourself without using a job title?
- What does being seen or valued mean to you now?

Reclaiming the self

One of the most important tasks of later life is crafting a new identity that reflects not just what a person has done, but who they are now. This includes reconnecting with inner traits, values, character strengths, and qualities like self-efficacy, resilience, creativity, or optimism, which continue to shape how retirement is experienced.

The Jungian turn inward

As we age, understanding who we are becomes more important than ever. Carl Jung wrote extensively on later life, including this reflection:

'Looking outwards has got to be turned into looking into oneself. Discovering yourself provides you with all you are, were meant to be, and all you are living from and for.'

Jung believed that the second half of life is not about building CVs or roles, it's about individuation or becoming more whole. That means embracing all of who we are: the parts shaped by culture and work, and the deeper parts we may have suppressed or postponed.

We don't need to accept a 'retired' identity unless we choose to. Instead, we can explore the person we are becoming.

A shift in coaching focus

For over 35 years, I've helped people understand themselves, mainly to help them be more effective at work. But in recent years, I've taken a different approach. Instead of helping people fit in with workplace expectations, I've supported clients in reconnecting with their natural style, their usual way of being, their authentic self.

This turn inward, towards inner development, is one of the most liberating shifts a person can make. Life becomes easier and more fulfilling when we stop performing and start aligning.

Variability in retirement experiences

Because identity in retirement is so personal, it helps to hear how others have made the shift. Here are some stories from clients I've worked with:

Sarah, who achieved career success early and had children later, felt energised at 60. With her children still at home, she had more in common with mums a decade or more younger than her and was ready for a new burst of activity.

John, a former police chief inspector, embraced fitness, cooking, and music festivals; activities he'd had no time for previously. At times, he became almost obsessed with his new pursuits, but they gave him a renewed sense of joy.

Carys, a senior university leader, retired early due to burnout. After reflection, she retrained as a holistic practitioner. She now works part-time and maintains a fulfilling balance between paid work and personal wellbeing.

And there are other stories, woven throughout this book.

These stories show the breadth of what's possible, and the importance of claiming a new identity that feels real and alive. As a coach, you can collect your own examples to share with clients who feel uncertain. Seeing what's possible in others helps them envision their own path.

> **Reflective practice: Reflecting on shifting identity**
>
> What new identity is your client beginning to claim, beyond labels and past roles?

The psychology of transition: Seven key factors

In my doctoral research, I reviewed over 12,000 studies and analysed 106 in depth. The final meta-analysis included data from nearly 11,000 participants and identified **seven psychological factors** that significantly influence how people adjust to retirement.

These are explored in much greater depth in my book *Rethinking Retirement*, but the overview is useful for coaches here:

- **Personality**: Traits like openness and conscientiousness shape how people plan, adapt, and engage with change.
- **Values:** Retirement often brings a shift in what matters. Clarifying values supports better life and career decisions.
- **Self-esteem:** Transitioning out of work can challenge one's internal sense of worth.
- **Self-efficacy:** The belief that 'I can handle this' is key to navigating uncertainty.
- **Mastery:** A sense of control helps reduce stress and improves wellbeing.
- **Social identity:** How connected people feel to groups and roles shapes both belonging and confidence.
- **Calling:** Having a sense of purpose beyond work can anchor identity and meaning.

Understanding where a client feels strong and where they feel depleted can guide your coaching focus. Some clients may need to rebuild confidence or agency, while others may be searching for a renewed sense of contribution or belonging.

> **The power of optimism**
>
> Research by Becca Levy shows that having a positive outlook can extend life expectancy by over seven years. Encourage clients to cultivate a growth mindset and challenge pessimistic narratives.

For coaches wanting to go deeper, each of these factors is unpacked with tools and insights in my book *Rethinking Retirement: For Positive Ageing*.

> **Reflective practice: Coach reflection in practice**
>
> If you've introduced the seven psychological factors, which ones feel strongest for your client, and where is support most needed?

The role of relationships

Encouraging a holistic life review

While clients may come to coaching with work or purpose-related goals, it's important to take a broader perspective, especially in later life. Meaning doesn't come from work alone. We also need connection, belonging, and community.

Work is often where people form most of their friendships. It's the context in which they share stories, celebrate wins, vent frustrations, and feel seen. When work ends, those connections often fade, despite good intentions to stay in touch. That's why helping clients think proactively about relationships is so important.

Relationships in later life

Encourage clients to explore their current social landscape:

- How many of their friends are still from the workplace?
- Have they started building new circles before leaving work?
- Are they involved in any groups, clubs, or volunteering activities?

Making new friends in later life isn't always easy. It requires intention and sometimes courage. Clients may need reassurance that it's normal to feel awkward, and that finding your people takes time. Not every group will be the right fit, and that's okay. Part of this work is helping clients identify where they feel a natural sense of belonging.

It's also helpful to encourage diversity in friendships:

- A friend who shares a hobby or pushes you to show up to a class when you'd rather stay in.
- A confidant you can talk to about life's real stuff.
- Someone whose energy lifts you up and helps you feel alive.

- Intergenerational friends; people who stretch your perspective or spark a different kind of joy.

And a gentle reminder for clients to reflect on their own role in relationships. Are they open, curious, and energising to be around, or have they unknowingly fallen into the role of the 'energy vampire'? These are subtle but vital conversations.

The power of relationships: Insights from the Harvard study

The Harvard Study of Adult Development, now over 85 years in progress, has become a foundational resource in understanding human flourishing. Its most consistent finding is both profound and practical: strong relationships are the single most reliable predictor of long-term happiness and health (Waldinger & Schulz, 2023).

As coaches, this finding challenges the tendency to over-focus on productivity, income, or achievement in later life. While these can remain meaningful, we must help clients reclaim and rebuild social connections as part of their career transition.

The study's associate director, Dr Marc Schulz, frames this through the lens of 'social fitness', the idea that our relational wellbeing needs the same regular care and attention we give to physical health. Especially for clients retiring from structured environments, the loss of daily social contact can have emotional and even physical consequences.

In practice, this means helping clients explore questions such as:

- Who are the people they feel most themselves around?
- How are they maintaining or initiating regular contact?
- What activities naturally foster community or connection?

Many clients don't realise until they've left full-time work how much relational scaffolding was provided by the workplace. Career coaching, therefore, becomes not just a process of repositioning for income or activity but also of restoring social identity and connection.

>
> **Coach reflection prompt: Relationships and social fitness**
>
> **Where do relationships show up in your clients' career narratives, both as support and as absence?**
>
> How might you support them in building 'social fitness' alongside their next chapter planning?

Reclaiming time and rebalancing life

When work stops, clients gain back 40+ hours a week; often more if you count commuting or overtime. That sudden expanse of time can be both liberating and disorienting. While some of that space may go to household chores or rest, it's important to help clients consider how else they want to spend their time.

As coaches, we can encourage a broad exploration of possibilities:

- Movement and physical activity.
- Creative or practical pursuits.
- Continued learning.
- Quiet time, nature, and solitude.
- Volunteering or community involvement.
- Time with family, friends, and pets.

We can help them balance structured activities (classes, appointments, commitments) with flexible pursuits (reading, gardening, spontaneous outings). The goal isn't to fill every hour, but to create rhythm, variety, and joy.

As clients reclaim time once filled with work, it's helpful to explore how that time can support deeper connection, with others, and with themselves. Some clients may benefit from mapping how they spend their time now and identifying where relationships or community could play a bigger role. I expand on this in the section 'Rebuilding Rhythm: Structure and Routine' later in this chapter.

COACHING TOOL 4.3: The relationship wheel: Mapping connection and belonging

In later life, relationships often shift. Work friendships may fade, family dynamics change, and it's common to feel a mix of connection and disconnection. This exercise helps clients take stock of their current social world and identify where they want to grow or reconnect.

Step 1: Introduce the concept

Explain that this exercise is about mapping connection, not judging it. The goal is to notice who's present in their life, and who might be missing.

You might say:

'Let's explore your current social landscape. Where do you feel connected? Where is there joy, support, or depth? And where might you want to build more connection?'

Step 2: Create or use the Relationship Wheel

Provide clients with a blank wheel or a version with labelled segments. You can include categories such as:

- Fun and laughter
- Deep Talk and emotional support
- Mutual care
- Creative collaboration
- Shared interests
- Local community
- Intergenerational connection

Encourage clients to:
- write the names of people who fit in each category;
- reflect on how full or empty each segment feels; and
- notice which areas bring energy, and which ones feel thin or missing.

Step 3: Reflect and act

After completing the wheel, ask reflective prompts like:

- What do you notice when you look at your wheel?
- Where are you well-supported?
- Where might you want more connection, or different kinds of connection?
- Are there people you'd like to reconnect with, or new circles you'd like to explore?

Encourage small, manageable steps, joining a group, reaching out to someone, or saying yes to a new opportunity.

Chapter 4: The Psychology of Retirement and Identity Shifts

Coaching tip:

For visual learners, this tool can be especially powerful. It externalises their social world, helping clients name both abundance and absence, and to take intentional steps towards richer connection.

Work provides not just identity, but social connection. That absence often hits harder than expected. By helping clients reflect on their social landscape, take action to build new relationships, and consciously shape their time, we're equipping them for a richer and more resilient life stage.

Coaching prompt: Mapping connection after work

'Who are your people? And who do you want to be spending more time with?"

This prompt helps clients reflect on their current relationships, identify gaps or longings, and make intentional choices about connection and community in later life.

You might also ask:

- What relationships feel nourishing, and which feel draining?
- Where are you finding belonging right now?
- Who do you miss, and who might you like to reconnect with?

Talking with a partner: Are your visions aligned?

Whether a client is retiring, shifting into part-time work, or pursuing something more values-led, these decisions often ripple beyond the individual. If they are in a relationship, it's important to consider how their partner's expectations, hopes, or financial situation may influence the path ahead.

Some couples discover they have very different ideas about what this next stage looks like. One may want to downshift; the other may be at their career peak. One might picture more time together; the other might be craving space and reinvention. Sometimes, both want to reduce their income at once, but haven't planned for how that will work financially or emotionally.

As coaches, we don't need to resolve these dynamics, but we can prompt the conversation.

> **Coaching prompt: Talking with a partner**
>
> **'Have you talked with your partner about what this next chapter looks like, for both of you?'**
>
> *This prompt helps bring unspoken assumptions into view and invites deeper, more collaborative planning for the next stage of life.*
>
> Encourage clients to reflect on shared rhythms, finances, and expectations. You might also explore:
>
> - What kind of lifestyle do you both want, and is it financially and emotionally sustainable?
> - Are you aligned on work, time, space, and pace, or are there points of tension?
> - What needs to be negotiated to move forward with clarity and mutual respect?

Navigating internalised ageism

While we will explore workplace ageism and structural issues in Chapter 8, it's important to acknowledge internalised ageism, the unconscious adoption of society's limiting views about ageing.

Many clients arrive with quiet, self-limiting beliefs:

- 'I'm too old to change.'
- 'No one wants someone my age.'
- 'It's too late to start something new.'

These narratives don't arise from nowhere; they're shaped by cultural messages absorbed over decades. Even confident, competent people can carry internal scripts that restrict what they believe is possible in later life.

> **Reflective practice: Exploring beliefs about ageing and retirement**
>
> For the coach: What beliefs do you hold about ageing and retirement? How might these shape the coaching space you create?
>
> For the client: What age-related messages might be limiting their view of what's possible, and are those beliefs really true?
>
> *Ask: 'What have you absorbed about people your age doing this kind of work?'*

This simple reframing can be powerful. Often, it opens the door to deeper questions about choice, agency, and possibility.

Encourage clients to replace outdated narratives with more flexible and empowering ones. Challenge assumptions about what later life *should* look like, and create space for what it *could* look like.

Resilience and health planning

No matter how thoughtful the planning, life after full-time work doesn't always unfold as expected. Health issues, caregiving responsibilities, or sudden loss can derail the most optimistic vision of later life.

This is where resilience coaching comes into its own. We're not just helping clients dream, we're helping them stay grounded, adaptable, and well-resourced in the face of change.

As a coach, you can support clients to:

- Create flexible, realistic plans.
- Develop a 'Plan B' mindset: What if things change?
- Build emotional strength to navigate the unexpected.

> **Coaching prompts: Resilience and health planning**
>
> *These prompts help clients prepare for uncertainty without fear. They encourage flexible thinking, emotional readiness, and the ability to adapt if life takes an unexpected turn.*
>
> You might ask:
>
> - If your plans had to change tomorrow, what would your next best option look like?
> - What if health deteriorates or caregiving responsibilities arise, how might your plans shift?
> - What could support you in staying resilient, grounded, and well-resourced in a changing future?

COACHING TOOL 4.4: Plan B mapping

Helping clients prepare for the unexpected:

Later life rarely unfolds in a straight line. Even the most carefully crafted plans can be disrupted by health changes, caregiving responsibilities, bereavement, or shifts in energy and priorities. While we can't predict the future, we can help clients explore what flexibility looks like, and consider a Plan B (or even a Plan C) that still aligns with their values.

Why it matters:

Clients often arrive in coaching with a clear picture of how they hope things will go. But unexpected life events, such as illness, financial change, or family needs, can upend these expectations. Rather than ignoring this possibility, we can gently open space for alternative scenarios and responses.

Case example:

James had carefully mapped out a phased glide into consultancy work, but a sudden triple bypass changed everything. His focus shifted overnight: from career to wellbeing, from legacy projects to deeper connection with his family. Coaching helped him reframe what mattered and find peace with a different kind of impact.

Using this in coaching:

- Invite clients to reflect on: 'What if things don't go to plan?'
- Use gentle language to explore possible disruptions without catastrophising.
- Help clients articulate alternative routes that would still feel meaningful.
- Reframe Plan B as not a failure, but as another version of success.
- Encourage clients to identify resources (internal and external) they could draw on if circumstances change.

Reflection prompts for clients:

- If something disrupted your current plans, what would matter most to hold onto?
- What else might be possible, something smaller, slower, or different?
- Who or what would help you adapt?
- How can you build flexibility into your vision now, so you're less shaken if change comes?

Coaches don't need to fix or predict what's ahead, but we can build the mindset and tools to help clients respond to life's curveballs with more confidence and grace.

Purpose in later life

Purpose in later life doesn't have to mean productivity. It's not about achieving, performing, or proving, it's about contribution, creativity, connection, and legacy.

Coaching prompt: Purpose in later life

'I want to be remembered for . . .'

This prompt invites clients to reflect on what truly matters, not in terms of roles or achievements, but through the lens of values, impact, and presence.

You might also ask:

- What kind of difference do you hope to make, even in small ways?
- What stories do you want others to share about how you lived or showed up?
- What would it mean to leave a quiet legacy, rather than a grand one?

For some clients, purpose will take the form of creative projects. For others, it's about volunteering, mentoring, or simply showing up for the people they care about. The key is to experiment, try new roles, revisit old passions, and imagine futures aligned with their values.

For some clients, especially those leaving behind long-held roles or identities, the challenge isn't just what to do next; it's how to feel that life still matters. As existential psychologist Steven Heine writes, meaning is often found through connection: to people, community, purposeful work, and something larger than oneself. Heine's **Meaning-in-Life Audit** is a simple but powerful tool to help clients explore where their current sources of meaning are strong, and where they may need attention.

This is a theme I explore in more depth in my forthcoming book *Olderhood Unfolding*, out in 2026, where I focus on life beyond full-time work, and how people rediscover meaning through joy, contribution, and deeper self-connection.

ARTHUR, 62: A NEW LENS ON LIFE

Arthur, a former marketing director, had always been drawn to music. In his 60s, after leaving the corporate world, he started taking photos at local gigs, initially as a way to get closer to the music, but soon it became something more. He taught himself editing techniques, built relationships with venue owners, and eventually began writing short reviews for an independent music blog.

What began as a hobby became a path of rediscovery. One of his photo essays helped a young, unsigned artist land a support slot on a national tour. It reminded Arthur that his creativity still had an impact. 'I didn't go looking for purpose', he said. 'But maybe it found me anyway.'

Coaching reflection: Purpose in later life doesn't always begin with a master plan. It often emerges when joy, skill, and curiosity are allowed to meet.

Coaching tip:

Not everyone has an Arthur-style passion waiting in the wings, but joy and meaning often appear when clients stay open, experiment, and notice what feels right in real time.

Reflective practice: Exploring purpose and contribution

What does purpose mean to your client now, and how might they experiment with new expressions of it?

COACHING TOOL 4.5: Finding purpose

Inspired by Arthur's story of discovering purpose through unexpected passions.

Many people believe they need a grand plan for their next chapter. But often, meaning emerges through following what feels joyful, engaging, or creatively satisfying, as it did for Arthur.

This exercise invites your client to explore how joy, curiosity, and contribution might guide their next steps.

Step 1: Track what energises you

Ask your client to reflect on their recent weeks.

- What activities made you lose track of time?
- When did you feel most alive, creative, or absorbed?
- What sparked curiosity, even something small?

Step 2: Reflect on joyful contribution

Now shift from what you enjoy to how it affects others.

- Have you shared a talent or interest that helped someone else?
- When have you received appreciation or seen impact from something you enjoyed doing?
- What small acts felt surprisingly meaningful?

Step 3: Spot the threads

Encourage them to look for links between what brings joy and what creates a sense of contribution.

- What patterns are emerging?
- Are there overlooked interests or passions that might lead somewhere new?

Step 4: Let go of the plan (for now)

- If you set aside expectations or 'should', what would you explore more of?
- What might happen if you simply followed what energises you for a while?

Rebuilding rhythm: Structure and routine

Time after retirement can feel both expansive and disorienting. Without the structure of a work week, some clients feel unmoored or unmotivated.

This is where rhythm matters. Not rigid scheduling, but intentional structure that supports energy, joy, and purpose.

> **COACHING TOOL 4.6: Time mapping exercise**
>
> Invite clients to explore two key questions:
> - How do you currently spend your time?
> - How would you like to spend your time?
>
> This comparison often reveals what's missing, what's working, and what they want more of. It also encourages clients to become more conscious of how time either nourishes or depletes them.
>
> Encourage clients to:
> - balance structured activities (classes, volunteering, appointments) with flexible pursuits (reading, gardening, rest);
> - plan for variety and energy management;
> - notice patterns: what energises, what drains?;
> - try small shifts, like adding one new thing a week.
>
> This isn't about staying busy. It's about building a week that feels meaningful and alive.

> **Reflective practice: Life review and meaning-making**
>
> What does a good week look like for your client, and how can they shape time to support joy and wellbeing?

Closing reflections

Retirement is far more than a financial or logistical decision, it is an emotional and identity-rich transition that often prompts deep reflection on meaning, purpose, and self. As coaches, we hold space for that exploration, supporting clients as they navigate who they are beyond their professional roles.

This work requires an approach that is as individual as the clients we serve. Life stage, health, financial circumstances, and shifting goals all shape the retirement experience. Our role is to meet people where they are, gently encouraging reflection, experimentation, and the creation of new routines that support wellbeing and purpose.

At the same time, we must be willing to challenge the internalised ageism and limiting beliefs that can cloud this period of life. By helping clients reshape their narratives, towards contribution, legacy, and self-defined success, we empower them to move forward with confidence and clarity.

In the next chapter, we'll explore how clients can design fulfilling post-work lives, including volunteering, lifelong learning, and reimagining daily rhythms that support joy, connection, and continued growth.

Reflective practice: Exploring beliefs about ageing and retirement

What are your beliefs about retirement and ageing? How might these beliefs influence the way you coach clients in later life? Are you modelling a positive, open mindset about ageing in your own life and work?

In a nutshell

- Retirement is often a non-linear, emotionally rich experience, not just a financial event.
- Identity, self-worth, and structure shift when work ends: how to support that transition.
- Generativity, purpose, and legacy all play a role in shaping a meaningful later life.
- Challenging internalised ageism and fostering a growth mindset are important.
- Practical tools can help with identity review, legacy reflection, time mapping, and resilience planning.

Chapter 5
Designing a meaningful life after full-time work

> **Summary**
>
> *This chapter supports career coaches in guiding clients through the transition beyond full-time work. Rather than viewing retirement as an endpoint, it introduces a life design approach grounded in rhythm, curiosity, and personal meaning. Coaches are offered practical tools, such as time mapping, reflective prompts, and conversational strategies, to help clients explore this stage of life with clarity, intention, and openness. It encourages a mindset of experimentation and alignment, recognising that meaning unfolds differently for each individual. It also introduces the ThriveSpan model as a broader framework for later-life wellbeing and purpose, which will be explored in greater depth in a future book.*

The shift from career to life design

Leaving full-time work marks the end of a role, but not the end of contribution, growth, or engagement. For many clients, the question is no longer, 'What job will I do?' but rather, 'What kind of life do I want to create now?'

Retirement is often framed as a full stop: a period of withdrawal or endless leisure. But in practice, most people want more than that. They want rhythm. They want connection. And above all, they want meaning.

This chapter helps career professionals support clients in designing a fulfilling life after full-time work, whether or not paid work continues to play a part. It's about moving from career design to life design: rethinking time, purpose, contribution, and identity in ways that feel alive and authentic.

As one client put it: 'I'm not done; I'm just starting in a different way.'

Reflective practice: Exploring purpose and contribution

How comfortable are you exploring non-work goals with clients? Do you include purpose, time use, and joy in your coaching conversations?

A path through meaningful later life

As clients step into life beyond full-time work, many encounter questions that don't have quick answers.

- Who am I without my role?
- What matters most now?
- What kind of life do I want to shape next?

There's no single path through these questions, no checklist for a meaningful later life. But there are patterns worth noticing: shifts in rhythm, values, contribution, and curiosity that can offer guidance.

Rather than prescribing a fixed plan, coaching in this stage invites exploration. Each client will move at their own pace, testing what fits, letting go of what no longer serves, and discovering what gives meaning now.

Rediscovering purpose and value

Clients leaving structured employment often wrestle with a loss of productivity and identity. For decades, their days were shaped by tasks, responsibilities, and external validation. Now, they're asked to imagine a meaningful life without titles, targets, or deadlines. For some, that feels freeing. For others, it can be unsettling.

Purpose in this phase often softens and expands. It becomes less about achievement and more about resonance. Some clients are drawn to mentoring, caregiving, creative expression, or activism. Others find purpose in presence: showing up for a friend, tending a garden, or simply being more available in family life.

What matters is not the extent of the act, but its alignment with values. Coaching can help clients name and honour forms of contribution that aren't tied to a payslip or prestige, yet are no less valuable.

Coaching prompt: Discovering your inner drive

'What do you care about enough to give your time to it, even if no one expects you to?'

This prompt invites clients to reflect on intrinsic motivation, values, and self-directed purpose.

EVELYN, 65: A TABLE SET FOR BELONGING

After retiring from a healthcare career, Evelyn missed casual conversation and the rhythm of being needed. She posted a handwritten note in her local library: *Coffee and conversation, Thursdays at 10. All welcome.* That small act sparked a weekly gathering. 'We all just needed a reason to show up', she said. In helping others belong, she found her own renewed sense of meaning.

SUNIL, 67: A QUIET CONTRIBUTION

Sunil didn't want to join groups or lead anything. But he noticed a local footpath was overgrown and began clearing it quietly each week. Passers-by started to nod, smile, and thank him. 'It's nothing big', he said, 'but it feels good to do something useful, quietly'. Coaching helped him see this small, steady act as a valid and valued contribution.

Purpose and brain health in later life

Recent longitudinal research adds a compelling dimension to our understanding of purpose. A 10-year study (Pfund et al., Psychological Science, 2024) tracking over 1,700 adults aged 65+ found that a strong sense of purpose was linked to greater cognitive resilience. Even more telling: those experiencing cognitive decline reported a sharper drop-in purpose than in overall life satisfaction. Purpose, in this light, is not just motivational; it's neuroprotective.

The researchers define purpose not as a lofty life mission, but as personally meaningful goals and directions. Micro-moments of mattering, feeling useful, engaged, or connected may be key. As coaches, we can invite clients to explore:

- Where do you feel most alive or useful?
- What brings energy or quiet fulfilment?
- How might these small clues shape the next chapter?

Purpose doesn't have to be grand. It has to be felt.

Time, rhythm, and the reshaping of days

Time changes shape after full-time work ends. The familiar scaffolding of the working week: Monday meetings, deadlines, Friday wind-downs, dissolves. Some clients try to replicate that structure with detailed plans. Others drift, surprised by how disorienting open time can feel.

This temporal void isn't a failure; it's a natural adjustment. After decades of externally imposed rhythm, clients may need space to experiment, recalibrate, and rebuild a flow that suits who they are now. As coaches, we're not here to replace one schedule with another. Our role is to support rhythm, not rigidity, grounded in values, energy, and the season of life they're in.

> ### COACHING TOOL 5.1: Time mapping for meaning
>
> ***Exploring how time use reflects values and energy***
>
> This tool helps clients gain awareness of how they currently spend their time, and how that aligns (or doesn't) with what feels meaningful. It shifts the focus from productivity to *life rhythm*, energy flow, and emotional fulfilment.
>
> **Step-by-step:**
>
> 1. **Sketch the current week**
>   Invite clients to draw or map out a typical week, not just appointments and tasks but also:
>   - energy highs and lows;
>   - time alone versus with others;
>   - moments of joy or connection;
>   - obligations (e.g. caregiving, admin); and
>   - activities that feel draining or nourishing.
> 2. **Reflect and discuss**
>   Explore what stands out. Is their time aligned with what they value? Are they overcommitted in some areas and undernourished in others?
> 3. **Imagine a more meaningful rhythm**
>   Encourage them to sketch a second version: a rhythm that feels more spacious, energising, or aligned.
>
> **Reflection prompts:**
>
> - What would you like more of in your week?
> - What would you release or reduce if you could?
> - What's missing entirely that you crave?
> - Where might you start, even with one small change?
>
> **Use it when:**
>
> - Clients feel stuck, busy, or unfulfilled.
> - A new phase of life is beginning (e.g. retirement, caregiving, semi-work).
> - You're exploring energy, wellbeing, or life balance.
>
> This isn't about planning; it's about awareness.

Coaching prompt: Reclaiming your rhythm

'What small shift would make your week feel more like your own?'

This prompt helps clients identify gentle, achievable changes that restore a sense of agency, rhythm, or alignment in daily life.

PAMELA, 54: REIMAGINING RHYTHM

After her career in visual styling ended abruptly, Pamela retrained as a postpartum doula. 'It's not the career I expected', she said, 'but it's deeply aligned'. Her new rhythm centres on care, calm, and presence.

DAVID, 69: FINDING FLOW IN SPACIOUSNESS

David, a former engineer, initially filled every day with tasks: DIY, volunteering, courses. But he felt oddly restless. In coaching, he reflected: 'I think I've been trying to outpace the emptiness.' He began creating 'unscheduled space' in his week, time for reflection, wandering, reading. Over time, that unstructured time became the most nourishing.

Clients often need permission to experiment with rhythm, especially when they've been conditioned to equate time with productivity. Help them design weeks that honour both energy and meaning, with enough spaciousness to breathe and adapt as life evolves.

Social connection and the quiet drift

Work brings built-in social interaction. Colleagues, casual conversations, office banter, shared breaks, it all forms a web of connection that's easy to take for granted. When that ends, clients may suddenly find their days quieter, their world smaller. Many are surprised by how lonely, invisible, or unanchored they feel.

Even clients who identify as introverts or enjoy solitude often report a sense of disconnection. Friendships drift. Shared purpose dissolves. The regular rhythm of being seen and needed fades.

As coaches, we can gently invite clients to reflect on what types of connection nourish them now, not just out of habit, but out of alignment with who they are becoming. Rebuilding connection at this life stage often means being more intentional, more discerning, and sometimes more courageous.

COACHING TOOL 5.2: Social circle mapping

Bringing awareness to relationships and connection needs

This tool helps clients visualise the structure and quality of their current social world. By mapping out different layers of connection, they can reflect on who matters most, where energy is gained or drained, and what forms of connection they may be seeking more of in this life phase.

Step-by-step:

1. **Draw a three-circle map**
   Invite clients to sketch three concentric circles:

   - **Inner circle** – close confidants, trusted loved ones
   - **Middle circle** – regular contacts, friends, neighbours, workmates
   - **Outer circle** – broader acquaintances, groups, social media, clubs

2. **Populate the circles**
   Encourage clients to place people in whichever circle feels right, using initials or symbols if privacy helps.

3. **Reflect together**
   Discuss what stands out. Invite the client to explore:

   - Who energises and uplifts you?
   - Who do you miss, or want to see more of?
   - Where are the gaps?
   - What new forms of connection might be welcome now?

Why it matters:

Later-life transitions often reshape social worlds through retirement, relocation, bereavement, or shifting priorities. This simple exercise can uncover feelings of isolation, overlooked support, or forgotten joy. It also offers a starting point for intentional reconnection or building new relationships.

> **Coaching prompt: Strengthening meaningful connection**
>
> 'What small step could you take this month to connect with someone meaningfully?'
>
> *This prompt encourages intentional connection, helping clients nurture relationships that matter and reduce social drift.*

MARTIN, 67: A WALK WITH INTENT

Martin realised he hadn't had a real conversation in days. 'I miss just bumping into people', he said. On impulse, he joined a local walking group he'd seen advertised in the library. 'It wasn't deep chat', he said, 'but it felt good to be among others again'. That weekly walk became a quiet anchor and the start of new friendships.

Clients don't need to rebuild their entire social life at once. One lunch. One group. One message to an old friend. Often, reconnection begins not with a breakthrough but with a simple showing up.

Contribution and the value of unpaid work

When paid roles fall away, many clients struggle to name their contributions. Their sense of worth may have been closely tied to formal work, job titles, or financial productivity. Without these markers, some wonder: *Am I still useful? Do I still matter?*

Yet many continue to give in powerful ways, supporting others, caring for family, mentoring quietly, or holding emotional space for those around them. These roles are often undervalued by society and by clients themselves.

Coaching can help uncover these acts of significance. Contribution doesn't have to be prestigious or public. It just needs to feel *meaningful and aligned.*

COACHING TOOL 5.3: Contribution inventory

Recognising how we give, and where it matters most

Contribution isn't always formal or visible. This tool helps clients reflect on the full range of ways they give to others: emotionally, practically, creatively, or quietly behind the scenes. It's particularly helpful for clients navigating identity beyond paid work or struggling to name what they *offer* now.

Step-by-step:

1. **Explore the full spectrum of giving**
   Invite clients to list or map the ways they contribute. Use the following categories as a guide; not all will apply, and others may emerge:
   - **Emotional support** – being present, listening, encouraging
   - **Practical help** – caregiving, running errands, tech support
   - **Creative expression** – sharing art, music, writing, ideas
   - **Community involvement** – volunteering, activism, mutual aid
   - **Quiet reliability** – showing up, being dependable, holding space

2. **Reflect and reframe**
   Help clients recognise the value in what they give, even if it is unpaid, unnoticed, or taken for granted.
   - Which forms of giving feel most energising or grounding?
   - Are any beginning to feel draining or unbalanced?
   - Where might more boundaries be helpful?
   - Are there ways of giving that they'd like to reengage with or explore?

Why it matters:

People often downplay their contributions if they're not tied to a role, salary, or title. This tool validates informal, relational, and creative forms of giving and helps clients reconnect with a sense of meaning and impact.

Coaching prompt: Noticing your everyday impact

'Where are you already making a difference, and how does it feel?'

This prompt invites clients to recognise their existing impact and connect with the emotional rewards of contribution.

> ### FARAH, 61: A QUIET ARCHIVE
>
> Farah, newly semi-retired, attended a lecture on women's suffrage and began volunteering at a local archive. 'I thought I was just attending a talk', she said. 'Now I feel part of something that matters.'
>
> ### ROSA, 70: THE STEADY SUPPORT
>
> Rosa never thought of herself as 'contributing' in retirement. But as she described her week, it emerged that she cooks weekly for her sister, helps neighbours with shopping, and babysits her grandson most Fridays. 'It's just what I do', she said. Coaching helped her see the quiet generosity in those routines and to name it with pride.

Saying no

Sometimes, clients take on too much in an effort to stay useful. They may struggle to say no to requests from family or community, fearing it means they're being selfish or underutilised.

Coaching can help clients distinguish between contributions that **nourish** and contributions that **deplete**. You might ask:

- *Which of your current roles feels sustaining? Which feels obligatory?*
- *What would it mean to contribute from energy, not guilt?*
- *Is there something you'd like to pause, pass on, or renegotiate?*

Affirm that contribution in later life is most meaningful when it's **aligned, chosen, and life-giving,** not when it's driven by pressure or performance.

Growth through mentoring

Mentoring is not just about giving back; it's a pathway for personal growth and renewal. In later life, becoming a mentor can reignite curiosity, sharpen communication skills, and provide rich opportunities for emotional and relational development.

Whether mentoring professionally or informally, the act of guiding others invites us to reflect on what we've learned and how we express it. It reinforces purpose, strengthens intergenerational bonds, and cultivates a mindset of active engagement with the world.

Three key areas of growth through mentoring include:

- **Emotional intelligence:** Mentoring enhances self-awareness, empathy, and the ability to hold space for another's growth.
- **Active listening:** Great mentors ask questions, listen with curiosity, and resist the urge to fix or advise too quickly.
- **Simplicity in communication:** Sharing knowledge with clarity and humility fosters deeper connections and trust.

Mentoring is not a one-way street. It offers as much to the mentor as to the mentee, renewing a sense of value, legacy, and relevance.

Coaching prompts: Learning by guiding

- How might mentoring be a new avenue for your own growth?
- Who might you learn from, even as you guide?
- What strengths or experiences could you offer someone just starting out?

Creativity, curiosity, and new joys

Clients may rediscover interests long set aside. Others may draw a blank when asked what they enjoy. After decades of work, caregiving, or responsibility, curiosity can go quiet. It takes time, and permission, to reawaken.

Curiosity doesn't need to lead to a big project or identity shift. It's enough that something is noticed at the edges of attention: a flyer in a café, a book long left on the shelf, an old passion stirring again.

This kind of exploration is often non-linear. It might begin with a single session, a walk through a gallery, or an afternoon dabbling. Coaching can invite clients to follow what *intrigues* them, not what they're good at or known for.

It's not about mastery. It's about play, openness, and becoming more alive.

Coaching prompts: Rekindling curiosity and forgotten joys

Use these prompts to help clients reconnect with buried interests, early passions, or quiet sparks of curiosity that may have been set aside over time.

- What have you always been curious about, even just a little?
- What's one small step you could take this month to follow that interest?
- What did you enjoy before work or family life crowded it out?

KWAME, 72: THE WHISPER OF WORDS

Kwame, a retired builder, was drawn to a poetry anthology. He began writing. Nervously at first, then more confidently. 'I never thought I had anything to say', he shared. 'But poetry helped me understand things I'd never put into words.'

AMINA, 64: THE JOY OF TRYING

Amina joined a local ceramics class after seeing a flyer in a café. 'I hadn't touched clay since school', she laughed. Her first bowl collapsed. So did the second. But by week four, she was absorbed. 'It's not about what I make', she said. 'It's about how I feel while I'm doing it.'

Clients don't need to know their 'thing'. They just need space to notice what sparks a flicker of interest, and the encouragement to take one step towards it.

When life shifts unexpectedly

Even the best-laid plans may be reshaped by health changes, caregiving responsibilities, or financial disruption. A client may have pictured travel, creative projects, or a purposeful 'next act', only to find themselves adjusting to new limits or demands they didn't choose.

These moments can be profoundly disorienting. Clients may grieve the loss of a hoped-for later life, feel guilty for resenting their circumstances, or question their own resilience.

Coaching in this space is not about solutions. It's about presence: supporting emotional honesty while holding open the possibility of adaptation and renewal. Clients often need to hear: *You're allowed to feel what you feel. You're also allowed to change your vision.*

Resilience here isn't about pushing through. It's about **softening into flexibility**. What else could later life become?

Coaching prompts: Navigating change with clarity

These reflective questions support clients in making peace with shifting realities while staying anchored in purpose and possibility.

- What has changed, and what still matters most to you now?
- What parts of your vision still feel possible, even in a new form?

FARID, 68: THE QUIET PIVOT

Farid had planned to launch a consultancy after decades in international development. When his wife was diagnosed with a degenerative illness, he let those plans go. 'I thought I'd lost everything', he said, 'but this season holds its own meaning'. He now volunteers part-time with a carers' network and finds pride in being present through difficulty.

RUTH, 66: REBALANCING AFTER DIAGNOSIS

Ruth had been gearing up for a travel-filled retirement when she was diagnosed with a chronic illness. 'It was like the map disappeared', she said. Coaching helped her shift focus to local joys: her garden, photography, and a small memoir project. 'It's not the life I planned', she shared, 'but it still feels like *mine*'.

Clients don't need a perfect Plan B. They need support to revise with grace, to stay connected to what matters even when the terrain changes. Your role is not to steer but to walk beside them as they find new footing.

Life as prototype: Small experiments, big shifts

When clients face uncertainty about purpose, contribution, or identity, there can be a strong urge to 'figure it all out'. But big commitments can feel overwhelming or premature.

That's where experimentation comes in. Small, low-risk trials allow clients to test ideas, explore interests, and notice what energises them, without pressure to get it right.

This approach, borrowed from design thinking, is especially powerful in later life. It supports discovery over decision and movement over stuckness.

You don't need a full plan. You need a place to begin.

Types of low-stakes experiments might include:

- shadowing someone in a role or setting of interest;
- trying a short course, workshop, or drop-in group;
- volunteering for a limited time or one-off event;
- adjusting daily rhythm, e.g. adding creative time or a walking habit; and
- hosting something informal: a book group, conversation circle, or lunch.

The goal isn't mastery. It's insight.

Coaching prompts: Experimenting with possibility

These prompts encourage clients to take gentle, exploratory action, helping them learn through doing, without pressure to get it 'right'.

- What's one low-stakes experiment you'd like to try in the next few weeks?
- What might you learn, not just about the activity but about yourself?

> **ALAN, 64: ONE AFTERNOON AT THE MARKET**
>
> Alan was curious about working with food, but unsure if it was realistic post-retirement. He offered to help a friend run a farmers' market stall one Saturday. 'I didn't expect much', he said, 'but I came home buzzing'. That single afternoon nudged him towards a part-time seasonal role that now structures his week and feeds his joy.
>
> Experiments reduce pressure, build momentum, and offer clarity. They allow clients to engage not just with what they *think* they want, but with what actually feels right when lived, even briefly.

A word on joy

Joy isn't a luxury; it's an anchor. Especially in later life, small moments of joy can stabilise, uplift, and reconnect. They act as emotional ballast when roles shift, health changes, or the future feels uncertain.

Yet joy is often overlooked in coaching, seen as frivolous compared to 'purpose' or 'goals'. Clients may downplay it too, especially if they've spent years equating worth with work.

But joy is not a distraction from meaning. It's one of its deepest sources.

Joy doesn't have to be loud or performative. It can be found in

- music that stirs memory;
- time in nature;
- making something by hand;
- shared laughter or gentle touch;
- moving the body freely; and
- moments of beauty or awe.

Coaching can invite clients to tune into what feels nourishing, not just productive, and to create more space for those experiences.

Coaching prompts: Making space for lightness

These prompts invite clients to notice the small joys and subtle lifts in their emotional landscape and to create more room for what nourishes.

- What brings you lightness, and how can you make more space for it?
- When did you last feel quietly delighted or emotionally lifted?

LUCYNA, 69: JOY IN THE GARDEN

After losing her husband, Lucyna felt lost. One day, she began tending her long-neglected garden. 'It gives shape to my days and colour when everything else feels grey', she said. Her joy didn't arrive with fireworks but with quiet growth.

RHYS, 62: DANCING INTO THE WEEKEND

Rhys joined a Friday evening dance group on a whim. 'I hadn't danced since my twenties', he said. 'Now it's the highlight of my week.' The movement, the music, the shared rhythm, all of it reminded him he was still very much alive.

Joy isn't optional in later life; it's essential. And often, it leads clients not away from purpose, but towards it.

Closing reflections

Life after full-time work isn't a retreat. It's an invitation.

- An invitation to reimagine time.
- To rediscover purpose.
- To reconnect with joy, contribution, and self.

This stage of life isn't simply about what clients will do next; it's about who they are becoming. The shift is less about goals and more about alignment. Less about plans and more about presence.

Your role as a coach is not to deliver a master plan, but to walk alongside your clients as they navigate this unfolding. To witness uncertainty without rushing resolution. To hold space for meaning to surface in its own time.

Some clients will want structure. Others will want spaciousness. Some will leap towards reinvention. Others will inch towards reconnection. Your job is not to decide the pace but to honour the path.

'What now?' becomes less of a problem to solve, and more of a question to live into.

The ideas in this chapter are part of a broader exploration of how we shape meaningful lives beyond full-time work. From my work with hundreds of clients, a framework gradually emerged, not as a fixed model, but as a gentle guide for reflection.

I call it the ThriveSpan model. ThriveSpan is not a prescription. It's not a timetable or a checklist. It's a path of possibility, one that each person walks in their own way, at their own pace.

I developed this model to support reflection after full-time work, a stage when identity, purpose, and rhythm often begin to shift. Work may still feature, but it's no longer the centre. Something deeper wants to emerge.

The model invites exploration of nine elements, grouped into three themes:

- **Self and wellbeing** (your personal foundations).
- **Connection and contribution** (relationships and impact).
- **Exploration and fulfilment** (growth and joy).

Each person finds their own rhythm within it.

ThriveSpan is introduced here only in outline. It will be explored more fully in my next book, *ThriveSpan: A New Map for Meaningful Later Life*, a deeper resource for both individuals and later-life coaches.

For now, this chapter offers a practical bridge, helping clients reorient their time, reconnect with meaning, and step into possibility with care and curiosity.

Chapter 5: Designing a Meaningful Life After Full-Time Work

 **In a nutshell**

- Help clients reframe purpose beyond productivity and status.
- Use tools to explore rhythm, energy, time, and meaningful activity.
- Honour each client's pace: some will seek structure, others spaciousness.
- Offer exercises like time mapping, identity reflection, and curiosity prompts.
- Adapt sensitively around health, loss, caregiving, and shifting priorities.
- Let questions guide insight, alignment, and personal meaning.
- Stay reflective in your use of tools, presence, and timing.
- This chapter offers a bridge towards ThriveSpan, a broader framework for meaningful later life.

Chapter 6
Practical tools for career coaches

> **Summary**
>
> *This chapter presents a practical toolkit for career coaches working with midlife and later-life clients. Drawing on psychological insight and lived coaching experience, it offers structured yet flexible tools for exploring identity, purpose, energy, and life design. The chapter also introduces adaptive practices for working with emotional complexity, such as grief, caregiving, and health shifts, and emphasises reflective, ethical use of tools that honour each client's context and pace.*

The role of tools in midlife and later-life career coaching

Career coaching in midlife and beyond requires a nuanced, flexible approach that reflects the complexities of ageing, identity, and transition. Tools and exercises provide both structure and focus, yet they must be applied with sensitivity to each client's unique life context. Whether a client is navigating a sudden redundancy at 52, seeking a new direction at 60, easing into retirement at 67, or seeking meaning at 74, the tools in this chapter are designed to support deep reflection, practical action, and hopeful reinvention.

In this chapter, we'll explore a range of coaching tools, from reflective exercises to structured audits, and provide guidance on adapting these tools to the specific challenges and opportunities of later life. The aim is to empower you as a coach to help clients rediscover their identity, purpose, and potential, even as they navigate the emotional and practical realities of life transitions.

While some tools have already been introduced in earlier chapters where they naturally supported the narrative, this chapter brings together a set of core coaching resources designed to form the bedrock of your practice with clients in midlife and beyond. We'll include practical and engaging tools such as values clarifiers, time use mapping, and skills translation exercises to deepen your work and spark meaningful dialogue with clients.

Reflective practice: Introducing tools with intent

Think about your own coaching practice: How do you currently decide when to introduce a tool in a session? What assumptions do you bring about how much structure your clients need, and where might flexibility serve them better?

Foundations of effective coaching tools

Before we dive into specific tools, it's important to reflect on *why* these particular ones have been chosen and how they differ from more general coaching exercises. You likely already have your own trusted toolkit; what follows are tools selected for their particular relevance to midlife and later life, shaped by the psychological, social, and existential dimensions of ageing.

Reflective practice: Assessing tool relevance

Pause to consider: how well do your current tools meet the needs of clients in midlife and later life? Where might more adaptation or emotional sensitivity be needed?

These foundations inform how we select and use tools effectively:

Adaptable and person-centred (e.g. Tool 6.6: Energy and Time Use Audit, Tool 6.8: Designing a Week)

Coaching in midlife and later life requires a flexible, responsive approach. Tools must be adaptable to suit diverse aspirations, circumstances, and energy levels. Both you as the coach and the client using tools on their own should feel confident in modifying, expanding, or simplifying exercises to suit the individual's story, interests, and pace.

Grounded in psychological insight (e.g. Tool 6.5: Roles and Identity Mapping, Tool 6.13: Legacy Interview)

These tools are chosen for their ability to support core psychological needs at this life stage: reinforcing identity, autonomy, meaning, and agency. When tools validate a client's lived experience and affirm their strengths, they create a safer foundation for growth, reinvention, or reflection.

Sensitive to context (e.g. Tool 6.10: Health and capacity)

Ageing brings unique life contexts, including health changes, caregiving responsibilities, loss, and evolving social roles. Effective tools do not ignore these realities but work with them. They honour both the constraints and the possibilities of later life.

Ethical and empowering (all tools are framed as invitations, not prescriptions)

All tools should reinforce client autonomy. They are offered as invitations, not directives. The client remains the expert in their own life, and our role as coaches is to provide thoughtful support, not solutions.

These foundational principles will help you assess not only which tools to use, but *how* and *when* to use them, ensuring they serve your client's evolving needs with respect and insight.

Reflective practice: Tool alignment and adaptation

Reflect on a recent session with a client in midlife or later-life. Which tool or approach did you use, and how well did it align with their needs, energy, and context? If you could adapt it to better suit them, what might you change?

(St)Age-specific coaching approaches

In this section, we focus on three later-life coaching stages; not based on age, but on lived experience and emotional readiness. These are:

- **Reappraising and repositioning:** When clients begin questioning past paths and exploring change (often in their 50s).
- **Rebalancing and redefining:** When identity, caregiving, or health shifts reshape priorities (typically in their 60s).
- **Reimagining and reconnecting:** When clients seek meaning beyond paid work through contribution, creativity, and legacy (often in their 70s and beyond).

Each of these stages is supported by coaching tools and reflective frameworks that help you meet clients where they are.

One 55-year-old might be actively pursuing promotion; another might be quietly contemplating a new way of living. A 70-year-old might be reawakening creatively just as a 62-year-old feels lost after leaving work.

These aren't age-based stages but reflective coaching lenses, useful for attuning to emotional readiness and life context rather than chronology.

What follows is not a rigid typology, but a flexible framework to help you tune into the lived realities of mid and later life. These (st)ages reflect common transitions many clients face: emotionally, practically, and psychologically. They can be fluid, overlapping, and experienced at different times, depending on context.

Reappraising and repositioning
(Often experienced in the 50s, or when clients begin to question the path they are on.)

This is a stage of *anticipation*, often marked by professional restlessness or the desire to pivot. Clients may be reflecting on what they've built, and whether it still fits. Some are navigating redundancy; others want more autonomy or flexibility. It's also a time when the first glimmers of legacy begin to surface.

- **Focus**
  - Career reinvention, skill repositioning, or preparing for a shift in pace.
  - Managing energy, burnout, and ambition in new ways.
  - Encourage possibility thinking and curiosity about 'what's next'.
- **Common (st)age frames**
  - The awakening phase.
  - Seeking new ground.
  - Chapter of anticipation.

Suggested tools:

- **Tool 6.1** (Life Timeline): *Especially relevant during the awakening phase, when clients reflect on how past transitions shape present identity.*
- **Tool 6.2** (Translating Skills): *Useful during the chapter of anticipation, where clients begin to imagine future directions.*
- **Tool 6.3** (Values Clarifier): *Fits well in the seeking new ground frame, as clients reassess what matters most.*

Rebalancing and redefining

(Often experienced in the 60s, or when identity and priorities begin to shift more fully.)

This is one of the most emotionally complex stages. Clients may feel pulled between winding down and starting anew. Some are caring for others or managing health concerns. Others feel a renewed desire to contribute, but in a more values-led or time-flexible way. Grief, relief, and growth often coexist here.

- **Focus**
  - Transition planning, identity redefinition, caregiving, burnout recovery.
  - Help clients let go of old narratives while staying open to reinvention.
- **Common (st)age frames**
  - Bridging identities.
  - The unfolding phase.
  - Chapter of transition.

Suggested tools:

- **Tool 6.4** (Retirement Mindset): *Supports clients navigating the chapter of transition, especially when emotions are mixed.*
- **Tool 6.5** (Roles and Identity Mapping): *Helpful during the unfolding phase, as identity shifts and new roles emerge.*
- **Tool 6.6** (Energy and Time Use Audit): *Resonant with the bridging identities stage, where daily rhythms and roles may be in flux.*
- **Tool 6.10** (Health and Capacity): *Essential during the unfolding phase, when energy levels and caregiving often influence planning.*

Reimagining and reconnecting

(Often experienced in the 70s and beyond, or when work is no longer central to identity.)

This stage is rich with possibility, but often underexplored. Clients may no longer be in paid work, yet many are actively creating, learning, mentoring, or contributing in new ways. This is a time of deep expression, where inner life, community, and legacy take centre stage.

- **Focus**
  - Rediscovering purpose, creative expression, deepening relationships, reflecting on meaning.
  - Use gentler, spacious tools that allow for reflection, reconnection, and celebration.

- **Common (st)age frames**
  - The flourishing phase *(a later-life stage focused on expression, purpose, and connection beyond traditional work roles)*.
  - Living authentically.
  - Chapter of expression.

Suggested tools:

- **Tool 6.11** (Creative Expression Prompts): *Encourages expression during the chapter of expression or the flourishing phase.*
- **Tool 6.13** (Legacy Interview): *Especially meaningful in the living authentically frame, where story and wisdom come to the fore.*
- **Tool 6.12** (Joy Mapping): *Helpful during the flourishing phase, when clients reflect on joy, peace, and emotional wellbeing.*
- **Tool 6.14** (Interesting Inventory): *Resonates with the chapter of expression, encouraging cognitive engagement and personal richness.*

As a coach, your skill lies in tuning into your client's unique rhythm. These (st)ages aren't a prescription, but an invitation to listen more deeply to the transitions beneath the surface and to choose tools that meet them where they are.

> **Reflective practice: Using the reappraising–rebalancing–reimagining lens**
>
> Reflect on your current clients. Which of the three (st)ages: reappraising, rebalancing, reimagining do you most often encounter? How might this lens help you fine-tune your tool selection or language in future sessions?

Core coaching tools and exercises

On the following pages you will find detailed descriptions of 14 practical coaching tools, complete with purpose, step-by-step instructions, and guidance on when and how to use each one effectively. These tools are adaptable across life stages and can be tailored to fit the client's emotional landscape, energy levels, and goals. These are followed by seven further practices to consider.

Chapter 6: Practical Tools for Career Coaches

COACHING TOOL 6.1: Life timeline exercise

This tool supports identity exploration and reflection on life transitions, aligning with psychological insight and emotional sensitivity.

Purpose:

To explore life themes, identity evolution, and key transitions in a client's journey.

Instructions:

- Ask the client to draw a horizontal timeline across a sheet of paper.
- Mark significant life events, transitions, accomplishments, and periods of high or low energy.
- Discuss patterns, recurring themes, pivotal moments, and their emotional significance.
- Reflect together on what they might want to carry forward, or consciously leave behind.

Use:

Ideal in early sessions, especially when clients feel uncertain about identity or stuck in past narratives. It lays the groundwork for self-awareness, reframing, and deeper meaning-making.

Clients in acute grief may need gentler narrative tools first (e.g. Tool 6.15 – Emotional Validation, or Tool 6.17 – Gentle Narrative Work).

Pair this with

- **Tool 6.5** (Roles and Identity Mapping) helps connect past transitions with present identity.
- **Tool 6.13** (Legacy Interview) to deepen reflection on life themes.

COACHING TOOL 6.2: Translating skills and experience worksheet

This tool reinforces agency and helps reframe accumulated experience, aligning with empowerment and adaptability.

Purpose:

To help clients reframe their accumulated experience and identify skills that can be applied in new or evolving contexts.

Instructions:

- List key skills, roles, and career or life experiences.
- For each, ask: What does this enable? What does it demonstrate? Where else could it be used (e.g. mentoring, consulting, volunteering, creative projects)?
- Identify transferable competencies and explore potential areas for growth or contribution.

Use:

Especially useful when clients are considering reinvention, unretirement, or sector shifts, this tool builds confidence and opens up new pathways by showing how the past remains relevant.

Clients who feel low in confidence may need affirming narrative work first (Tool 6.17 – Gentle Narrative Work).

Pair this with

- **Tool 6.3** (Values and Priorities Clarifier) helps ensure skill redirection aligns with current priorities.
- **Tool 6.7** (Work–Life Grid) visualises how future roles might fit into life design.

COACHING TOOL 6.3: Values and priorities clarifier

This tool clarifies core motivations at this life stage, aligning with person-centred practice and psychological insight.

Purpose:

To surface what matters most at this life stage and to align choices with core values.

Instructions:
- Offer a list of values or use a values card deck (custom or pre-made).
- Invite the client to sort these into 'most important', 'somewhat important', and 'less important'.
- Facilitate a reflective discussion on how well their current life aligns with top values and what may need adjusting.
- Optional: Revisit this over time to track shifting priorities.

Use:

Effective as a mid-process tool or during periods of transition, it offers clarity and focus when clients are evaluating future options or making major decisions.

Overwhelmed clients may need simplified values lists or visual methods (e.g. cards or colour sorting).

Pair this with

- **Tool 6.6** (Energy and Time Use Audit) compares time use with values alignment.
- **Tool 6.9** (Purpose and Contribution Cards) brings values into action through non-vocational roles.

COACHING TOOL 6.4: Retirement mindset assessment

This tool surfaces hopes and fears about retirement, aligning with context sensitivity and ethical practice.

Purpose:

To explore and challenge attitudes towards retirement, surfacing both hopes and fears that influence decision-making.

Instructions:

- Present a series of statements related to retirement (e.g. 'I'm excited about slowing down', 'I worry about losing purpose', 'I look forward to having more control over my time', 'I fear becoming irrelevant').
- Ask clients to rate their agreement with each statement using a Likert scale (e.g. 1 = strongly disagree to 5 = strongly agree).
- Invite discussion on the reasons behind each rating.
- Explore areas where a mindset shift might support greater freedom, joy, or confidence.

Use:

Ideal for clients approaching retirement or feeling ambivalent about it, this tool opens up a balanced conversation about both anticipation and apprehension.

Avoid with clients who are still in active career exploration and are not yet contemplating retirement.

Pair this with

- **Tool 6.7** (Work–Life Grid) for practical planning.
- **Tool 6.9** (Purpose and Contribution Cards) to explore post-retirement purpose.

A printable version of this exercise is available in the resources toolkit online. To access, scan the QR code or visit the web address at the start of this book.

COACHING TOOL 6.5: Roles and identity mapping

This tool expands the client's self-concept and supports identity reinvention, aligning with psychological insight and adaptability.

Purpose:

To explore the client's broader identity beyond professional roles and uncover neglected or emerging aspects of self.

Instructions:
- Ask the client to list all the roles they currently identify with (e.g. parent, friend, partner, artist, grandparent, neighbour, volunteer).
- Invite them to indicate which roles energise them, which feel obligatory or draining, which are fading, and which they might want to grow or rediscover.
- Map these visually if helpful, grouping them into themes or life domains.

Use:

Useful for clients navigating identity loss, role transitions, or the 'emptiness' that can follow retirement, it opens space to reframe who they are in a more expansive, human way.

Avoid with clients who may feel emotionally vulnerable; validate their emotions before mapping.

Pair this with
- **Tool 6.1** (Life Timeline) connects identity to personal history.
- **Tool 6.14** (Interesting Inventory); sparks curiosity about emerging roles.

COACHING TOOL 6.6: Energy and time use audit

This tool promotes sustainable time use and wellbeing, aligning with context sensitivity and empowerment.

Purpose:

To build awareness of how time is used and how energy is spent or replenished across daily activities.

Instructions:

- Ask the client to track a typical week's activities, noting both time spent and how energised or depleted they feel after each one.
- Use a simple rating system (e.g. +2 = highly energising, 0 = neutral, −2 = highly draining).
- Reflect together on what patterns emerge. Which activities restore them? Which are obligations or energy drains?

Use:

Supports clients in redesigning their routines for sustainability, vitality, and better alignment with personal priorities, especially during transitions.

Avoid overloading the client with data if they're in emotional fatigue; simplify the tracking.

Pair this with

- **Tool 6.7** (Work–Life Grid) translates insight into balance.
- **Tool 6.8** (Designing a Week) supports future rhythm.

COACHING TOOL 6.7: Work–life grid

This tool encourages intentional planning across life domains, aligning with adaptability and ethical practice.

Purpose:

To help clients visualise and rebalance their time across life domains such as work, rest, learning, creativity, connection, and contribution.

Instructions:

- Create a simple grid or pie chart with life domains (e.g. work, rest, learning, connection, contribution, play).
- Have clients estimate their current time or energy allocation in each area.
- Then, create a second version showing their ideal distribution.
- Discuss what shifts, small or large, might help move towards that ideal.

Use:

Especially helpful for clients at a crossroads – whether entering semi-retirement, juggling caregiving, or craving more balance in later life. It promotes intentional living rather than reactive time use.

Avoid pushing for balance too quickly; reflect on the emotional meaning of imbalance first.

Pair this with

- **Tool 6.6** (Energy and Time Use Audit) maps where time and energy are going.
- **Tool 6.3** (Values and Priorities Clarifier) explores alignment between values and time.

> **COACHING TOOL 6.8: Designing a week**
>
> *This tool builds autonomy and rhythm in daily life, aligning with empowerment and context sensitivity.*
>
> **Purpose:**
>
> To help clients envisage and test a weekly routine that reflects their current interests, energy, and lifestyle preferences.
>
> **Instructions:**
> - Ask the client to sketch out an ideal week, allocating time for rest, creativity, connection, movement, learning, and contribution.
> - Encourage them to reflect on what feels essential, joyful, or grounding.
> - Discuss what is realistically achievable and where small changes could be trialled.
> - Identify one or two new elements to experiment with over the coming weeks.
>
> **Use:**
>
> A supportive tool for clients transitioning out of full-time work or redefining how they use time. It helps create rhythm and structure with intentionality.
>
> Don't over-schedule; leave space for flexibility, rest, and exploration.
>
> *Pair this with*
> - **Tool 6.12** (Joy Mapping) identifies energising moments.
> - **Tool 6.10** (Health and Capacity) ensures sustainable routines.

COACHING TOOL 6.9: Purpose and contribution cards

This tool helps surface deeper meaning and non-vocational contributions, aligning with psychological insight and empowerment.

Purpose:

To support reflection on what purposeful living might mean now, and how clients might express this in everyday life.

Instructions:

- Provide a set of cards or a list of purpose-driven themes (e.g. 'Mentoring others', 'Creating art', 'Learning new things', 'Nurturing community', 'Making beauty', 'Being present for family').
- Ask the client to choose the cards or statements that resonate most.
- Facilitate a reflective discussion about why these stand out, how they show up in their lives, and what new forms they could take.

Use:

Ideal for clients seeking deeper meaning, especially in a post-work context. It encourages insight into non-vocational forms of contribution and engagement.

Not suitable for clients in acute transition who are struggling with basic self-worth; begin with stabilising tools.

Pair this with

- **Tool 6.1** (Life Timeline) reveals deeper purpose threads.
- **Tool 6.13** (Legacy Interview) connects purpose to legacy.

A printable version of the Purpose and Contribution Cards is available in the resources toolkit online. To access, scan the QR code or visit the web address at the start of this book.

COACHING TOOL 6.10: Health and capacity reflection tool

This tool honours physical and emotional realities, aligning with context sensitivity and ethical practice.

Purpose:

To integrate health, energy, and caregiving realities into planning, ensuring goals remain achievable and compassionate.

Instructions:

- Invite the client to reflect on their current physical and emotional capacity.
- Explore how energy levels fluctuate across the week or month.
- Discuss what boundaries, supports, or adjustments could protect wellbeing while still allowing growth or exploration.
- Consider pacing, rest, and delegation where needed.

Use:

Essential for clients managing chronic illness, fatigue, or other constraints, it ensures that aspirations remain rooted in self-care and realistic capacity.

Avoid over-focusing on limitations; include small wins and aspirations.

Pair this with

- **Tool 6.8** (Designing a Week) shapes realistic life rhythms.
- **Tool 6.6** (Energy and Time Use Audit) explores limitations and adjustments.

COACHING TOOL 6.11: Creative expression prompts

This tool enables emotional processing and insight through creativity, aligning with psychological insight and adaptability.

Purpose:

To tap into creativity as a pathway to insight, healing, or meaning-making, especially for clients feeling emotionally stuck or intellectually saturated.

Instructions:
- Offer the client one or more creative prompts such as:
  - Write a six-word story that sums up your current chapter of life.
  - Write a letter to your future self; five years from now.
  - Create a 'found poem' using words cut from magazines or newsprint that reflect your current emotions or hopes.
- Invite the client to read or reflect aloud on what emerges.
- Use gentle questions to explore underlying themes or shifts in tone.

Use:

Ideal for clients who enjoy journaling, self-expression, or need to bypass the analytical mind (when clients feel emotionally stuck or intellectually saturated). These prompts invite play, freedom, and a different kind of reflection.

Some clients may feel exposed by creativity; use gentle entry points and permission-giving language.

Pair this with

- **Tool 6.12** (Joy Mapping) brings emotional lightness.
- **Tool 6.17** (Gentle Narrative Work) supports deeper storytelling.

COACHING TOOL 6.12: Joy mapping

This tool supports emotional renewal and perspective-shifting, aligning with emotional sensitivity and psychological insight.

Purpose:

To help clients reconnect with moments of joy, appreciation, and emotional wellbeing, especially during periods of transition, uncertainty, or low mood.

Instructions:

- Ask the client to recall 5–10 moments in the past year when they felt joyful, peaceful, connected, or fulfilled.
- Plot these on a visual map, timeline, or mood board.
- Reflect together on patterns: What was present? Who were they with? What values or needs were being met?
- Identify how more of these elements could be consciously invited into their lives now.

Use:

A simple but powerful tool for emotional reset or perspective-shifting is particularly helpful when clients are focused on loss or limitation.

Avoid this if the client is not emotionally ready to access positive memories; offer validation first.

Pair this with

- **Tool 6.8** (Designing a Week) builds joyful elements into routine.
- **Tool 6.11** (Creative Expression Prompts) taps into emotional uplift.

COACHING TOOL 6.13: Legacy interview or audio memoir prompt

This tool affirms personal narrative and legacy, aligning with psychological insight and ethical practice.

Purpose:

To encourage storytelling, meaning-making, and reflection on personal impact, especially as clients move beyond traditional work identities.

Instructions:

- Frame this as an informal 'legacy interview' or personal memoir exercise.
- Provide a short list of prompts, such as:
  - *What do you want future generations to know about your life?*
  - *What moments are you most proud of?*
  - *What wisdom would you pass on to your younger self, or to someone coming after you?*
- Invite them to record themselves, write a few paragraphs, or share orally during the session.
- Reflect on how this process felt, and what surprised or moved them.

Use:

A deeply meaningful exercise for clients who are entering reflective life stages. It affirms that legacy isn't just about achievement, but about *connection, contribution,* and *story.*

Clients may find this emotional; provide time and space.

Pair this with

- **Tool 6.1** (Life Timeline) reveals key life threads.
- **Tool 6.9** (Purpose and Contribution Cards) draws connection to values.

> **COACHING TOOL 6.14: The interesting inventory**
>
> **A curiosity-driven tool for psychological richness**
>
> *Unlike earlier tools, this one is framed more as a practice than a worksheet, intentionally more fluid to invite curiosity rather than structure.*
>
> *This tool taps into curiosity and mental engagement, aligning with empowerment and adaptability.*
>
> **When to use this tool:**
>
> Use when clients feel stuck, under-stimulated, or unsure of direction. This tool works especially well when traditional goal-setting feels too rigid or heavy.
>
> Affirm that *interest* itself is valid; it doesn't have to be productive to be meaningful.
>
> Psychological richness arises not only from joyful experiences but also from challenging or emotionally complex ones, as long as they are interesting. Supporting clients to notice what stimulates their curiosity or makes them feel mentally engaged can become a powerful compass for life design.
>
> **Instructions:**
>
> - Invite the client to reflect on recent experiences that stirred their curiosity or made them feel 'alive' cognitively or emotionally.
> - Use prompts like:
>   - *What books, films, or conversations have captivated you recently?*
>   - *When did you last lose track of time because you were so engrossed?*
>   - *What's something new you'd like to try, not to master it, but to experience it?*
> - Encourage clients to intentionally design for 'the interesting', building later-life around engagement, not just goals.
>
> *Pair this with*
>
> - **Tool 6.14** (Interesting Inventory)
> - **Tool 6.8** (Designing a Week) puts 'interesting' into practice.

Supplementary coaching practices for later life

In addition to the structured tools described earlier, several approaches frequently appear in later-life coaching conversations. These are not always step-by-step activities but rather flexible practices that can be adapted to the client's emotional and narrative needs.

COACHING TOOL 6.15: Emotional validation activity

This tool helps normalise feelings during transitions, aligning with emotional sensitivity and ethical practice.

Purpose: To support clients in naming and normalising complex feelings, such as grief, resentment, or fear, especially in the early stages of transition.

Use: Invite clients to 'name the feeling without solving it'. Use scaling (1–10) or metaphor ('What weather is your mood today?'). Pause to validate before moving into planning.

Use when: Clients are emotionally raw, resistant to planning, or stuck in a narrative of loss. Don't rush to planning; allow time to process and normalise feelings first.

Pair this with

- **Tool 6.17** (Gentle Narrative Work) helps clients move towards meaning.
- **Tool 6.20** (Identity Anchors) stabilises identity during emotional turbulence.

COACHING TOOL 6.16: Role-based identity mapping

This tool expands the view of self beyond work, aligning with identity, support and psychological insight.

Purpose: To explore identity through life roles (e.g. parent, partner, worker, friend, volunteer).

Use: Ask clients to map current, fading, and aspirational roles. Use this to guide reflection on identity shifts and new opportunities.

Use when: Clients feel lost after a major role ends or when identity feels fragmented. Clients may feel shame around 'fading' roles; validate and normalise transition.

Pair this with

- **Tool 6.5** (Roles and Identity Mapping) deepens exploration across domains.
- **Tool 6.14** (Interesting Inventory) stimulates curiosity about future roles.

COACHING TOOL 6.17: Gentle narrative work

This tool supports meaning-making and emotional integration, aligning with psychological insight and emotional sensitivity.

Purpose: To help clients make meaning of their life stories, particularly after loss, retirement, or illness.

Use: Use prompts like 'Tell me the story of your last year', or 'What chapter are you in now?' Journaling or storytelling can support emotional integration.

Use when: Clients are reflective, grieving, or re-evaluating life direction. Some clients may fear being judged; emphasise that storytelling is for understanding, not performance.

Pair this with

- **Tool 6.1** (Life Timeline) helps structure story.
- **Tool 6.13** (Legacy Interview) affirms meaning and personal voice.

COACHING TOOL 6.18: Life review techniques

This tool helps uncover life patterns and values, aligning with context sensitivity and reflection.

Purpose: To look back meaningfully and identify themes, patterns, or values that can inform future choices.

Use: Use tools like the Life Timeline (Tool 6.1) in a deeper way, or explore 'turning points', proudest moments, and unfinished business.

Use when: Clients are looking for direction or meaning beyond productivity. Avoid rushing; this is a slow and often emotional process.

Pair this with

- **Tool 6.13** (Memoir Prompt) for deeper emotional closure.
- **Tool 6.19** (Legacy Projects) channels reflection into contribution.

COACHING TOOL 6.19: Legacy projects

Personal or creative acts that express a client's values and life wisdom, such as memoirs, letters, or mentorship.

This tool fosters creative contribution and impact, aligning with empowerment and ethical practice.

Purpose: To support clients in exploring their long-term impact, wisdom-sharing, or creative expression.

Use: Invite ideas like audio memoirs, letters to grandchildren, community projects, or artistic contributions.

Use when: Clients feel the pull to contribute or be remembered in meaningful ways. Don't assume clients want to create something; listen for the legacy they want to live, not just leave.

Pair this with

- **Tool 6.9** (Purpose and Contribution Cards) clarifies values.
- **Tool 6.12** (Joy Mapping) helps identify themes of meaning.

COACHING TOOL 6.20: Identity anchors

Stable aspects of self that persist across transitions; e.g. creativity, humour, caregiving, and curiosity.

This tool helps stabilise self-concept during change, aligning with psychological insight and emotional sensitivity.

Purpose: To reconnect with parts of the self that remain steady, even through change.

Use: Ask 'What part of you feels most constant right now?' or 'What identity has never left you?'

Use when: Clients feel unmoored, especially after career loss, health shifts, or relocation. Avoid assuming a fixed identity, this tool is about reassurance, not rigidity.

Pair this with

- **Tool 6.5** (Roles and Identity Mapping) makes anchors visible across roles.
- **Tool 6.6** (Energy and Time Use Audit) identifies energy-sustaining anchors.

> **COACHING TOOL 6.21: Curiosity-led exploration**
>
> *This tool supports experimentation and growth, aligning with adaptability and empowerment.*
>
> **Purpose:** To help clients follow interest and energy rather than rigid goals.
>
> **Use:** Encourage experimentation: taster courses, trial roles, volunteering, creative play. Let 'What's calling you?' guide your next steps.
>
> **Use when:** Clients feel under-stimulated, vague, or stuck in overthinking. This is a wandering phase; normalise trial and error, not outcome certainty.
>
> *Pair this with*
>
> - **Tool 6.14** (Interesting Inventory) identifies areas of interest.
> - **Tool 6.8** (Designing a Week) builds new experiments into routine.

Working with complexity

Coaching in midlife and later life often involves navigating layered, interwoven challenges. The tools in this chapter are designed to be flexible, but how and when you use them requires attunement to the client's emotional and practical context.

Health
Be prepared to adapt the pace, depth, or structure of exercises to match a client's fluctuating physical or mental capacity. Clients may not always disclose overwhelm directly, so build gentle check-ins into your approach. Pay attention to both verbal and non-verbal cues, and offer rest and reflection points as needed.

Loss and bereavement
Exercises like the Life Timeline or Roles and Identity Mapping can support clients in processing grief or major transitions. Encourage them to view these reflections as part of a broader life narrative, one that honours loss while also exploring what remains meaningful or possible.

Caregiving
For clients balancing caregiving responsibilities, tools like the Energy and Time Use Audit are especially valuable. They create space to clarify realistic commitments and can open up conversations about support, sustainability, and self-care.

Emotional readiness

Be attentive to emotional cues throughout your work. If a tool brings up unexpected intensity, allow space for that experience rather than rushing through. Clarify the purpose of each exercise in advance, agree on boundaries, and be willing to pause, slow down, or step back when needed.

> **Reflective practice: Honouring life complexity**
>
> Think back to a recent session where a client's life complexity, such as grief, illness, or caregiving, influenced the coaching dynamic. How did you respond in the moment? What signs did you notice emotionally or physically in the client, or in yourself? What might you adjust next time to better honour their needs and readiness?
>
> **Why it matters:**
>
> Later-life coaching often requires holding space for non-linear progress and layered emotion. Reflection like this supports ethical, responsive practice.

Integrating tools into the coaching journey

Integrating tools into your coaching practice involves more than simply selecting an exercise. Experienced coaches bring a reflective, responsive approach that adapts to each client's evolving story.

Select tools based on client stage and goal

Begin by assessing both the client's immediate concerns and their longer-term aspirations. For example, a client in their 60s may benefit from a combination of the Retirement Mindset Assessment and the Work–Life Grid, helping them navigate emotional readiness alongside practical planning.

Allow space for reflection and story-sharing

Encourage clients to articulate their experiences and insights as they engage with each tool. This deepens understanding, fosters trust, and builds self-awareness, often revealing layers of meaning beyond the exercise itself.

Combine tools to deepen insight

Strategic pairings of tools can generate powerful insight. For instance, using the Life Timeline Exercise alongside the Roles and Identity Mapping tool may help a client understand how past roles have shaped their present identity and open new possibilities for the future.

Invite feedback and co-creation

End sessions with reflective questions such as: 'What did you notice?' or 'What surprised you today?' These open-ended prompts turn each session into a collaborative process and offer valuable feedback for your coaching practice.

> **Reflective practice: Balancing structure and spaciousness**
>
> As you think about integrating tools into your own sessions: When have you trusted your instinct to pause, pivot, or stay with the story instead of using a planned tool? How do you balance structure and spaciousness in your coaching process?

Let's look at two examples:

THELMA, 62: ANXIOUS ENDING, INSPIRED BEGINNING

Thelma was approaching retirement after decades in a leadership role. She felt adrift, anxious about losing her professional identity and unsure of what life beyond work might look like. Through a combination of the Life Timeline Exercise and the Purpose and Contribution Cards, Thelma rediscovered a long-dormant passion for painting. This led to small but meaningful changes, carving out time for creativity each week, joining a local art group, and gradually building a new rhythm anchored in joy and self-expression. Over time, she began to see retirement not as an end, but as a chance to reimagine her identity on her own terms.

Coaching reflection: Clients may fear retirement as a loss, but coaching can help reframe it as creative reinvention, where identity evolves and dormant passions find new life.

EDDIE, 63: QUIET WORK IN A LOUD WORLD

Eddie, a quiet, introverted former librarian, struggled with visibility after early retirement. 'Everyone's shouting online', he said. 'I don't want to sell myself. I just want to be useful.'

Using strengths cards and drawing on principles from David Rock's *Quiet Leadership* model, we identified areas where his thoughtful, behind-the-scenes style was an asset.

He began indexing books for small publishers, then tutoring students with dyslexia. 'I never thought my skills would be in demand again', he said. 'But I've found my rhythm: slow, steady, and satisfying.' Eddie's story shows that later-life work doesn't need to be loud to be valuable.

Coaching reflection: Not all clients seek visibility or reinvention. Some look for work that matches their temperament, values, and pace. Coaching can help clients honour quieter strengths, uncover overlooked skills, and find roles where steady contribution is truly needed.

As you integrate these tools into your practice, consider the following questions to refine your approach:

- **Alignment**: Which tools feel most aligned with your clients' real needs and life stage?
- **Emotional depth**: Are you making room for emotional expression, not just goal-setting?
- **Comfort with uncertainty**: How comfortable are you with 'not knowing', and guiding clients through the ambiguity of change?
- **Tool selection criteria**: What guides your choice of which tool to use, and when?
- **Tracking shifts**: How are you noticing and supporting clients' psychological shifts, beyond external markers of success?

Reflective practice: Learning from what worked

Think back to a session where a tool worked particularly well, or didn't. What made the difference? How might your presence, timing, or choice of tool have influenced the outcome?

Adapting coaching questions for midlife and later-life clients

The power of questions in later-life coaching

While coaching tools provide structure and focus, the questions we ask, within and beyond those tools, shape the emotional depth and direction of the process. For midlife and later-life clients, questions take on particular significance. They must honour lived experience, surface emerging desires, and help navigate the emotional terrain of identity, freedom, loss, and renewal.

This section introduces six types of coaching questions, adapted for clients aged 50+, along with a set of reflective prompts and a brief exercise to help deepen your questioning practice.

Six coaching question types – adapted for later life

Type	Purpose	Example (later-life lens)	Tips for coaches
Open-ended	Encourage exploration and story-sharing	'What's becoming more important to you now?'	Start with what or how. Let clients lead. Avoid jumping too quickly to goals.
		'What does a meaningful week look like at this stage?'	
Closed	Clarify specifics or readiness	'Is this transition something you've been preparing for?'	Use sparingly. Useful for grounding the conversation or clarifying direction.
		'Do you feel ready to step back?'	
Hypothetical	Unlock imagination and shift perspective	'If age weren't a factor, what would you try?'	Ideal after exploring limiting beliefs. Helps release outdated narratives or assumptions.
		'What if you had a blank canvas for your next chapter?'	
Transformative	Prompt insight, shift mindset	'What belief about ageing might be holding you back?'	Watch for readiness. Use when trust is strong and clients are open to deeper exploration.
		'What are you learning about yourself in this season of life?'	
Rhetorical	Gently provoke or challenge thinking	'Isn't it curious how freedom can feel unsettling after years of structure?'	Use with care. Best when a client is already reflective or stuck in a limiting loop.
		'What if this is just the beginning?'	
Leading (avoid)	Steers clients towards your view, not theirs	'Wouldn't volunteering be a better use of your time now?'	Reframe to an open-ended style. Coaching is about curiosity, not persuasion.

Nine reflective coaching questions for later life

These can be used in-session or offered as journaling prompts between sessions. They support exploration of purpose, identity, possibility, and legacy:

1. What's calling you now, that didn't before?
2. What do you want to do with the freedom you have, or are creating?
3. What gives you a sense of aliveness?
4. What are you ready to let go of?
5. What's unfinished that still matters?
6. What kind of legacy or impact do you want to leave?
7. How do you want to spend your best hours now?
8. Who are your role models for this stage of life, and why?
9. What would it mean to honour this next life stage fully?

Reflective practice: Language and questioning style

Take a moment to consider your own use of language. Which types of questions come most naturally to you? How comfortable are you with silence, emotion, or questions that don't lead immediately to answers?

Closing reflections

Working with clients in midlife and later life is not simply about offering tools. It's about presence, patience, and perspective. These tools are not a prescription but a palette, designed to spark insight, honour complexity, and deepen client agency.

Your greatest skill is not in selecting the 'right' exercise, but in sensing when to offer structure, when to listen, and when to simply be with what's unfolding.

Some tools will land deeply. Others may not be right, at least not now. That is the art of later-life coaching: to meet each person where they are and to co-create a path forward grounded in respect, agency, and possibility.

Coaching tip:

Great coaching is not about having the perfect tool; it's about knowing when to offer it, how to hold space for what arises, and trusting the client to shape their own path.

 **Reflective practice: Evolving practice and stretch zones**

Take time to reflect on how your own coaching practice is evolving. Which tools resonate most with your way of working? Where do you feel called to stretch or experiment? And how might these tools become not just resources but invitations to deeper human connection?

Looking ahead

In the next chapter, you'll see these tools come alive through real client stories, from forced endings and quiet pivots to late-life reinvention and meaning-making after loss. These case studies offer a grounded look at how coaching unfolds in practice, and a fresh lens on your own stance, language, and presence when the path is uncertain.

 **Reflective practice: Confidence with new tools**

Take a moment to reflect on your own practice. Which tool from this chapter are you most drawn to? Which one do you feel less confident using, and why?

In a nutshell

- Tools offer structure, but must always honour the client's unique context and pace.
- Psychological insight, emotional sensitivity, and ethical practice underpin effective tool use.
- Tailor tools to life stage, not just age.
- Key exercises include life timelines, values clarifiers, identity mapping, purpose cards, and energy audits.
- Complexity is normal: be ready to adapt tools around health, grief, caregiving, or emotional readiness.
- Questions matter as much as tools; they shape insight, meaning, and client agency.
- Reflect regularly on your own tool choices, emotional presence, and use of questioning styles.

Chapter 7
Case studies: Navigating complex career transitions

> **Summary**
>
> *This chapter brings later-life transitions to life through composite, age-diverse case studies. Drawn from lived coaching practice, they explore the emotional, social, and practical dimensions of career change in midlife and beyond. Grouped thematically, from work-triggered shifts to identity-led reinvention, these stories illuminate the power of coaching to support meaning, agency, and renewal in later life.*

Introduction

Coaching clients in midlife and beyond requires nuance, empathy, and adaptability. While frameworks and models offer valuable structure, nothing illustrates the complexity of later-life transitions quite like real-world stories.

This chapter presents a series of composite case studies drawn from actual coaching engagements. Identifying details have been changed, but the emotional truths remain intact. These examples reflect the diversity of later-life experiences, from forced exits and voluntary reinventions to transitions shaped by life events such as illness, bereavement, or caregiving.

Grouped thematically, the case studies highlight different triggers and transition types, offering insight into how coaches can work effectively with a wide range of client needs.

Supporting clients after sudden job loss

When working with clients who have experienced abrupt or involuntary job loss, career coaches can draw from grief frameworks to provide structure and compassion. These clients may need more time, space, and emotional permission to grieve the loss before reimagining the future.

Tips for coaches:

- **Meet the client where they are:** Let them set the emotional tone.
- **Normalise grief responses:** Share that anger, denial, and numbness are common.
- **Offer community:** Encourage peer networks, alumni groups, or trusted circles that can act as a holding space.
- **Mark the transition:** Suggest ways to symbolically 'end' the role before planning what's next.
- **Stay present:** Regular check-ins and active listening matter more than quick solutions.

Transitions triggered by work and life disruption

Work-related transitions in later life are rarely just about jobs; they often involve layered emotional, social, and identity shifts. The following case studies reflect a variety of pathways: redundancy, health setbacks, caregiving pressures, and chosen reinvention. Each journey highlights how coaching can provide structure, validation, and renewed direction, even when the way forward feels uncertain.

ALAN, 61: REDUNDANCY, RESENTMENT, AND REINVENTION

Alan, an engineer, was made redundant after 35 years in a senior technical role. 'I gave them everything', he said bitterly. 'And now I'm on the scrapheap.' His identity was deeply tied to his expertise and loyalty. He initially rejected coaching, but after months of unemployment and job rejections, his wife encouraged him to try.

In coaching, Alan gradually moved from anger to cautiously exploring alternatives. We mapped his transferable skills and values, helping him reframe what he still wanted to contribute. He eventually pursued consultancy, supporting younger engineers and working part-time with a local college. What began as a reluctant stopgap became a fulfilling way to stay relevant, maintain dignity, and mentor the next generation.

Coaching reflection:

- Redundancy in later life often triggers grief, not just about the role, but about identity and future.
- Skill-mapping is valuable, but emotional validation and permission to feel angry are equally important.

- Reinvention isn't always glamorous; sometimes it's about stitching together dignity, utility, and hope.

MURIEL, 72: 'I FEEL INVISIBLE'

Muriel, a retired teacher and widow, came to coaching through a community centre. She felt her world shrinking after giving up volunteering: 'No one really notices me.' Beneath the loneliness was a deeper loss of status and being seen. 'I used to be someone people listened to', she said.

Coaching helped her reconnect with her values beyond old roles. When she mentioned a love of poetry, it became a spark. Muriel joined a writing group, then started a monthly intergenerational poetry circle at her library. 'I thought I had nothing left', she said. 'Turns out, I just needed a new way to matter.'

Coaching reflection:

- Older clients may not articulate 'career goals' but still need to feel seen, valued, and engaged.
- Coaching can help rediscover dormant passions and reframe later life as a time of expression, not exit.

DENISE, 64: FROM LEADERSHIP TO LETTING GO

Denise had held a senior leadership role in a large public sector organisation. She faced subtle pressure to retire early to make way for younger successors. 'No one says I'm too old', she said. 'They just stop including me.' She felt torn: intellectually engaged but emotionally bruised.

Coaching helped Denise unpack the tension between relevance and readiness. She feared losing status but was also exhausted. We explored what she wanted more of: less structure, more space, and time to write. She took phased retirement, negotiated a short-term project, and began a memoir-writing course.

Letting go of her executive identity wasn't easy, but coaching helped reframe it as a conscious, values-led transition. Denise later became a trustee for a national charity and mentored women in leadership.

Coaching reflection:

- Phased exits need support, both in negotiation strategy and identity recalibration.

- Loss of influence can hurt more than loss of income or routine.
- Mid-60s clients often straddle the tension between 'still capable' and 'ready for renewal', a subtle dance between pride and possibility.

TARIQ, 56: RE-ENTERING WORK AFTER A CAREER BREAK

Tariq had taken a five-year break in his early 50s to support ageing parents and manage his own health challenges. When he returned to the job market at 56, he was met with silence. 'It's like I fell off the planet', he said. Former colleagues had moved on, technology had changed, and his confidence had plummeted.

Coaching first focused on normalising shame, fear, and uncertainty. We rebuilt his career story around adaptability, responsibility, and wisdom gained through life experience. He revamped his LinkedIn profile, joined a mature jobseekers' network, and attended refresher training in finance operations.

Eventually, Tariq secured a flexible role with a small firm that valued his maturity and reliability. He also became a peer supporter for other men re-entering work after a time out.

Coaching reflection:

- Career breaks in midlife often attract stigma; coaching can reframe the break as a phase, not a failure.
- Confidence rebuilding is foundational, often before job search tools are introduced.
- Peer support and visibility matter, especially for men in their 50s and 60s, who are often underrepresented in return-to-work schemes.

GREGOR, 59: FORCED RETIREMENT DUE TO HEALTH

Gregor was a firefighter for over 30 years. At 55, after a serious injury, he was advised to retire on health grounds. 'I wasn't ready', he said. 'I thought I had five more good years. It's not just my job I've lost; it's my tribe.'

His case involved layered grief, loss of strength, routine, camaraderie, and service. Unstructured time left him 'drifting'.

Coaching began with permission to grieve and name what was lost. From there, we explored identity anchors: what remained when the uniform came off. Gregor had always mentored new recruits, so we explored options in training, public speaking, and youth education.

He eventually created a safety awareness programme for local schools and began volunteering with a veterans' charity. His physical limits remained, but his sense of usefulness returned.

Coaching reflection:

- Health-triggered exits can result in disenfranchised grief, loss without public recognition.
- Purpose and pride need to be redefined, not dismissed.
- Clients may need help adjusting to new energy rhythms, physical limitations, or uncertainty about what's next.

JULIA, 67: A LATE-LIFE SHIFT TOWARDS MEANING

Julia retired from a successful legal career at 63 but quickly became restless. After a few years of travel and leisure, she felt adrift. 'I've ticked all the boxes. Now what?' she asked. Though financially secure, she yearned for more purpose.

She came to coaching with no specific goal but a clear desire to contribute. Through values work, strengths cards, and curiosity-led exploration, Julia rediscovered her passion for the natural world and began volunteering at a rewilding project.

This sparked new momentum: speaking at community events, joining a citizen science initiative, and later enrolling in a part-time ecological restoration course. She described this chapter as 'a second adulthood, less about proving myself, more about being myself'.

Coaching reflection:

- Clients may not be 'lost' but under-stimulated, yearning for depth, connection, and challenge.
- Purpose isn't always about returning to work; sometimes it's about widening the field of engagement.
- Later-life shifts may benefit from experimentation rather than fixed outcomes.

ANNA, 51: CAUGHT OFF GUARD BY SUDDEN RESPONSIBILITY

Anna had worked part-time in admin roles while raising two children, never seeing her career as central. Her husband's high income meant she didn't need to push forward at work. 'I kept telling myself I'd get serious about my career later', she said. 'But later never came.'

At 51, her husband's poor health forced him into early retirement, and the financial burden shifted unexpectedly. For the first time, Anna had to earn enough to support them both. The shock was not just financial but emotional: 'I realised I'd never thought of myself as someone who could provide. And now I have to.'

She reached out for coaching, feeling both ashamed and angry at herself, at her past choices, and at a system that hadn't encouraged long-term financial independence for women. Coaching focused on reclaiming confidence, identifying transferable skills, and building a part-time return-to-work strategy. She updated her tech skills, explored short courses, and shifted her mindset from 'I've wasted time' to 'I'm rebuilding'.

Coaching reflection:

- Many women reach midlife with fragmented work histories and sudden financial responsibilities.
- Coaching can hold space for regret while building self-efficacy, offering structure, perspective, and hope when urgency feels overwhelming.

JANET, 68: STILL WORKING, STILL WORRYING

Janet had worked part-time in retail, hospitality, and care throughout her life, never staying long enough in one role to build a meaningful pension. Now 68, she received the state pension but little else. 'It's not enough', she said plainly. 'Even with help from my daughter, I have to work.'

She picked up shifts in a care home, though the work was exhausting. What worried her most wasn't energy; it was fear: 'If I can't work, I won't cope.' Retirement had never been about leisure; she just hoped it would feel safe.

Janet regretted not asking more questions earlier. 'I didn't know what I didn't know', she shrugged. Coaching focused on what she could control: finding lighter work, accessing pension credit, and exploring financial advice resources. Most importantly, we talked about meaning, what she still wanted this chapter of life to hold.

Coaching reflection:

- For clients like Janet, career coaching intersects with advocacy and access.

- Emotional support, practical referrals, and reframing work from survival to contribution can help restore dignity, agency, and a sense of possibility.
- Financial stress was a quiet thread in many of these stories. For more on this, see the coaching prompt on navigating financial realities later in this chapter.

MARY, 72: 'I THOUGHT I'D BE DONE BY NOW'

Mary was referred to career coaching by a local charity supporting older adults. Widowed five years earlier, she had gradually exhausted the modest savings she and her husband had set aside. Now 72, with only the state pension to rely on, she was struggling. 'I never thought I'd be looking for work at this age', she said quietly. 'I thought I'd be done by now.' Her voice carried no bitterness, just exhaustion.

Mary had spent most of her adult life raising children, supporting her husband's business, and working part-time roles: cleaning, reception, school dinners. There had never been much time, or money, for career planning. Now she found herself trying to cobble together enough income to stay afloat. The idea of re-entering the job market at 72 felt daunting. 'I don't even know what I can do anymore', she said. 'I'm not good with computers, my back isn't what it used to be, and half the time I feel invisible'.

As a coach, the first step was gently exploring her strengths and needs. Mary had warmth, reliability, and experience in spades, but also grief, fatigue, and a deep fear of rejection. Together, we identified low-impact roles in community centres and local schools, and she agreed to try a digital basics class through her library.

Coaching reflection:

- Clients like Mary challenge coaches to meet the intersection of age, poverty, grief, and self-doubt with both sensitivity and realism.
- Progress may be small, but helping someone regain a sense of agency, access support, or simply feel seen is profoundly meaningful.
- Not all coaching outcomes are about ambition; sometimes they are about stability, self-worth, and survival.

ELAINE, 67: RECLAIMING THE NARRATIVE

Elaine had spent over 30 years in a marriage where she managed the household while her husband built a successful consultancy. 'We made a choice', she explained. 'I supported him so he could go further, and he always said we were a team.' That narrative fell apart at 65, when their divorce was finalised and she discovered that the pension she thought they'd share was entirely in his name.

'I should have fought for a percentage of it,' she now says. 'The solicitor tried to talk about pensions, but I just didn't listen. I just wanted out.' The settlement was modest. Elaine had believed the house was paid off, only to learn that her husband had taken out a second mortgage during the downturn after Covid, without her knowledge.

Elaine had no choice but to return to work. She hadn't held a paid role in two decades. 'The last job I had was in a library before we had our first child', she said. 'I've volunteered, managed committees, raised three kids. But that doesn't translate easily to a CV.'

In time, her tone shifted. She began speaking not just about income, but about independence. 'I want to write the ending to my story, not have it handed to me', she said in our third session. Together, we explored flexible roles in education support, arts administration, and charitable fundraising, areas that tapped into her organisational strengths and natural empathy. Her confidence grew as we reframed her life experience as capability, not deficiency.

Coaching reflection:

- Divorce in later life often brings a double reckoning: emotional and financial.
- Coaching can help clients rebuild both confidence and clarity, especially when life hasn't turned out as expected.
- The shift from 'I have to work' to 'I choose to step forward' can be transformative.

Reflective practice: Coaching with financial awareness

How do you support clients navigating unexpected financial pressures with dignity and agency? What assumptions might you hold (or need to unlearn) about work, money, and stability in later life? How can coaching integrate emotional support and practical referral when finances are tight?

Transitions shaped by life events

Life events rarely follow a neat timeline. In later life, they often arrive in clusters: bereavement, divorce, relocation, changing family roles, disrupting not only plans but identity. In coaching, it's essential to meet the whole person, not just the 'career issue'.

These stories remind us that emotional shifts outside of work can spark powerful re-evaluations. Coaches working in this space must lead with presence, patience, and flexibility, allowing space for uncertainty before solutions are found.

SADE, 65: BEREAVEMENT AND THE SEARCH FOR WHAT'S NEXT

Sade retired at 63, planning to travel with her partner, but he died suddenly a few months later. 'Everything we dreamed of . . . it's gone', she said. 'Now I just exist.' Withdrawn and low in energy, Sade came to coaching tentatively after a friend's suggestion.

Rather than rushing into action, we started with gentle reflection: values journaling, nature walks, and permission to sit with the loss. Gradually, Sade felt drawn to volunteering at a local hospice. 'It felt like I could be useful again', she said.

This evolved into a peer support role for others facing grief. Coaching helped her pace her return to engagement, balancing self-care with contribution.

Coaching reflection:

- After bereavement, identity is often in pieces; coaching must start with presence, not pressure.
- 'What's next?' may take time; the process is relational, not transactional.

- Paid or unpaid work can become a healing practice, restoring connection and agency.

TOM, 62: DIVORCED, DOWNSIZED, AND STARTING OVER

Tom had recently divorced after 30 years of marriage. Adjusting to life in a small flat, he said, 'I feel like a visitor in my own life'. Work had once been his anchor, but he'd taken early retirement due to stress.

At first, Tom said he was 'done'. But in coaching, he began to realise it wasn't the job he missed; it was structure, community, and being useful. We rebuilt his weekly rhythm and explored energy-giving activities.

He started tutoring English to international students online, joined a men's walking group, and later developed a blog about navigating later life as a single man. These small steps rebuilt confidence and purpose.

Coaching reflection:

- Divorce can leave older men particularly socially and emotionally untethered.
- Career coaching in these moments may be less about employment and more about reconnection to identity, others, and structure.
- Micro-commitments (a class, a walk, a conversation) can act as lifelines.

NADIYA, 60: RELOCATION AND REINVENTION

After decades in London, Nadiya and her husband relocated to a coastal town for a slower pace of life. But once there, she felt disconnected. 'I thought I was ready for quiet', she said. 'But I miss the buzz.' Her career in arts education had ended with the move.

Coaching helped her rediscover community and influence. Nadiya joined a creative cooperative, ran workshops in local schools, and helped launch an intergenerational storytelling project. Later, she also began remote consulting for a former employer.

Coaching reflection:

- Relocation can trigger unexpected loss, not just of place but of identity and networks.
- Clients may need help navigating the space between the old self and the emerging self.
- Hybrid models of engagement, local volunteering, and remote work, can offer balance and belonging.

MARCUS, 68: FROM ACHIEVEMENT TO ALIGNMENT

Marcus, a former academic and consultant, had led a high-achieving life. He described his 60s as 'weirdly empty'. Despite a full CV and a long list of accolades, he asked, 'What now? Who am I if I'm not striving?'

He wasn't looking for another job, but he found it difficult to sit still. The absence of deadlines and recognition left him uneasy. In coaching, we explored where this discomfort came from. He realised he had long equated his value with output, that being useful meant being busy and productive.

Through journaling and reflective practice, Marcus began to notice where meaning was already present: in mentoring younger colleagues, in painting again after decades, and in slowing down enough to really listen, to himself and others. He later attended a mindfulness retreat and described his shift as learning to 'be with life, not just race through it'.

Coaching reflection:

- Clients may wrestle with identity when they are no longer busy or celebrated.
- Later life can invite a shift from achievement to presence, but this takes time and reassurance.
- Activities like journaling, art, or mindful mentoring can help clients reconnect with meaning beyond productivity.

When life throws you off course

Not all career changes are chosen. Sometimes life intervenes, suddenly or gradually, and the path you thought was solid begins to shift.

A health crisis. A partner's redundancy. The death of a parent. Investments that don't deliver, leaving savings more fragile than expected. Many midlife and later-life clients arrive in coaching feeling disoriented, not because they lack plans, but because their reality has changed faster than expected.

Some thought they were secure, only to discover the numbers don't stretch. Others feel ashamed that their 'sorted' life has unravelled. But this is more common than we acknowledge.

Career coaching in later life isn't just about finding new roles; it's about helping people find steady ground after sudden change. That means working holistically, with compassion for the whole person, not just their CV.

Identity-led transitions

Not all later-life transitions are driven by crisis. Some begin with a quiet sense of discontent, a growing awareness that the work or life that once fitted now feels wrong. Like wearing shoes on the wrong feet, there's discomfort without drama, a gentle but insistent nudge that says: This no longer feels like me.

These identity-led shifts are often slower, less visible, and deeply personal. They may emerge through questions like 'Is this still me?' or 'What haven't I done yet?'

Coaching in these moments is less about repair and more about reflection, experimentation, and conscious reinvention. These clients need space to explore identity, not just action plans.

> **ANYA, 60: FROM PROFESSIONAL TO POET**
>
> Anya had worked in marketing for over three decades. Her job was secure, her income comfortable, but she felt flat. 'I'm not unhappy', she said, 'just uninspired'. She had always written poetry in private but had never shared it.
>
> Through coaching, we explored what she was yearning for: expression, authenticity, and visibility. She began by attending open mic nights, then joined a writing group, and eventually published a small book of poems about ageing and reinvention.
>
> She later negotiated a four-day week, giving her more time to write, teach occasional workshops, and build a creative life alongside her professional one.
>
> **Coaching reflection:**
> - Clients may not want to quit their jobs, but rather to rebalance the ratio between duty and joy.
> - Creativity in later life is often less about career and more about voice, vitality, and freedom.
> - Coaches can help normalise the desire to 'come out' creatively, even if it feels risky or exposing.

DAVID, 66: REIMAGINING MASCULINITY IN RETIREMENT

David, a retired HR director, said, 'I thought I'd love retirement. Turns out I'm terrible at it.' He wasn't sure what he wanted, only that golf and gardening weren't enough. His wife joked that he was 'still in work mode' but with nowhere to go.

Coaching revealed a deeper desire: to explore different sides of himself beyond the roles of provider and professional. He'd always been curious about psychology and joined a men's group focused on emotional wellbeing.

Over time, David trained as a volunteer listener with a suicide prevention charity. He described it as 'the most meaningful thing I've ever done'. The shift wasn't about career; it was about expanding his self-concept.

Coaching reflection:

- Retirement can prompt identity questions, particularly around gendered expectations of achievement and usefulness.
- Sometimes, coaching is about helping clients name what they're longing for, even if they don't yet have the language.
- Inner transformation can be as fulfilling as outer productivity.

What these stories reveal about later-life coaching

These stories remind us that later life is not a winding down, but a turning outward, towards self, others, and the world in new and sometimes surprising ways. As coaches, our role is not to direct, but to accompany, to listen deeply, and to hold the space where clients can reflect, experiment, and reimagine who they are becoming.

Whether transitions are prompted by loss, restlessness, or the quiet call of renewal, our presence as coaches can make the difference between feeling adrift and feeling supported.

What these stories teach us (in practice)

- **Lead with empathy, not urgency.** Later-life transitions often unfold slowly and require psychological safety.
- **Expect ambiguity.** Clients may not begin with a clear goal; curiosity-led coaching can open the way.

- **Explore identity gently.** Many clients carry long-held assumptions about who they are or should be.
- **Broaden the lens.** Purpose, creativity, and contribution may matter more than paid work.
- **Normalise reinvention.** Change in later life is not always crisis-led; it may reflect growth, alignment, or readiness.

In a nutshell

- Later-life transitions are often complex, multi-layered, and emotionally rich.
- Change is not always career-led; it may follow illness, grief, caregiving, or quiet discontent.
- Clients often need space to grieve, reflect, and experiment before they act.
- Coaching must balance emotional presence with practical support.
- Identity work is central: clients are often redefining who they are, not just what they do.
- Purpose, creativity, contribution, and connection remain vital, often more so than income or status.
- Reinvention can be quiet, subtle, and deeply personal. Not every story is a dramatic transformation.
- Career coaching in later life is not about fixing problems; it's about walking alongside clients as they reshape meaning, identity, and belonging.

Chapter 8
Navigating ageism and changing workplace dynamics

> **Summary**
>
> *This chapter explores how career coaches can support clients to navigate age-related challenges in the modern world of work. From overt age discrimination to subtler forms of exclusion, it looks at how age intersects with other identities and how workplace norms have evolved, often leaving older clients unsure of their place. Through a focus on adaptability, confidence, intergenerational connection, health-related accommodations, and age-inclusive employer practices, this chapter offers both insight and practical coaching strategies to help clients stay visible, valued, and empowered at every stage of later life.*

A subtle and persistent bias

Ageism remains one of the most socially accepted and least challenged forms of workplace discrimination. While legislation has improved in recent years, negative assumptions about older workers persist, often unspoken, occasionally explicit, but almost always influential.

People in their 50s, 60s, and 70s too often find themselves sidelined, overlooked, or subtly edged out. Others internalise the cultural script that they should step back, slow down, or 'make room for the next generation'. These messages are not always overt; they appear in the language of 'fit', 'energy', or 'fresh thinking'. Ageism often hides behind a smile.

Yet the reality is that older workers bring deep expertise, loyalty, emotional intelligence, and resilience: precisely the qualities many organisations claim to value. This chapter explores how career coaches can support clients to navigate age bias, communicate their relevance, and make confident choices in changing work environments.

Beyond individual strategies, we'll also consider how organisational cultures are evolving, and how clients can identify workplaces that genuinely value experience and diversity across the lifespan.

Understanding ageism in context

Forms of ageism

There are different types of ageism; those of us who are older are aware of most of these. Younger people are often less so, and if working with an older age group, it is important to understand this. Ageism operates on multiple layers:

- **Explicit ageism**: Overt statements or actions, such as being told 'you're overqualified' or being excluded from promotion.
- **Implicit ageism**: Unconcious bias that results in subtle exclusion, lower expectations, or reduced opportunities.
- **Structural ageism**: Policies or workplace norms that disadvantage older employees, even without intent (e.g. tech-heavy hiring assessments, youth-focused branding, or lack of midlife training support).

It's important for coaches to understand and name these distinctions. Clients may sense something is 'off' but struggle to articulate it. Helping them name the pattern can be validating and empowering.

Ageism at the intersection

Age discrimination does not act alone. It intersects with gender, ethnicity, social class, and health status. A white male executive in his 60s may still hold cultural capital and networks that buffer against exclusion, while a working-class woman of colour the same age may be navigating layers of bias: age, class, ethnicity, and gender, all at once. Coaches need to understand how visible and invisible identities combine to shape opportunity, and to meet each client where they truly are. Let's look at Rita, Omar, and Len to understand more about their situations.

RITA, 55: CAREGIVER AND STARTING OVER

Rita had spent the last seven years caring for her mother with dementia. Before that, she worked in admin roles but never gained a formal qualification. At 55, with her caring responsibilities eased, she wanted to re-enter the workforce. 'I feel like I've been erased', she said. Employers saw the gap in her CV and overlooked the resilience, coordination, and problem-solving she'd been living every day. As a woman, she'd been taught not to 'oversell', and as someone from a working-class background, she wasn't used to asking for support. Coaching helped her reclaim her story, identify her strengths, and access a returner programme through a local health charity. It wasn't easy, but it was a start, not just to employment, but to self-recognition.

OMAR, 60: SKILLED BUT SIDELINED

Omar was a qualified engineer who had migrated to the UK from Syria a decade ago. Despite his technical skills and fluency in English, he noticed interviews often ended abruptly. 'They assume I'm out of date', he said. He was soft-spoken and meticulous, but colleagues sometimes mistook that for slowness. Age and accent, he felt, combined into a double barrier. Coaching helped him identify ways to showcase his recent training, reframe his quietness as thoughtfulness, and reconnect with an old mentor who helped him secure a part-time consultancy role. It restored more than income; it restored belief.

LEN, 62: NAVIGATING THE LONG SHADOW OF EXCLUSION

Len, a gay man, had worked freelance in the creative sector for most of his life. 'I've always had to fight to be taken seriously', he said. Now, with work thinning out, he wondered if it was even worth trying to compete. While outwardly confident, Len carried the legacy of years of coded exclusion, from early career discrimination to being passed over for leadership. Coaching created a space where he could voice that history and reconnect with what still mattered to him. He began mentoring LGBTQ+ creatives, offering what he once needed. The work gave him purpose and pride, without having to squeeze himself back into spaces that never quite fit.

Naming and challenging stereotypes

Clients don't arrive in coaching as blank slates. Many carry stories, not just from others, but from within, about what it means to be older in the world of work. Some are still pushing against tired tropes. Others have quietly started to believe them.

Understanding the myths helps dismantle them. Coaches can offer space to name, question, and gently reframe.

Common stereotypes about older workers

Despite decades of evidence to the contrary, certain assumptions persist:

- That older workers resist change.
- That they're less productive or less tech-savvy.
- That they're inflexible, slow, or too costly.

These narratives are often absorbed without question. Yet research consistently shows the opposite: older workers bring adaptability, emotional steadiness, and strong crisis management skills. They're often more loyal, more collaborative, and contribute to better team cohesion.

Coaching can support clients to gather and communicate the truth of their value, not defensively but with calm confidence. It might mean naming a recent learning experience. It might involve sharing examples of how they've supported change, mentored others, or introduced a useful tool or process. We can ask questions such as:

- 'What assumptions do you think others might make, and which simply aren't true for you?'
- 'What real-life story might gently challenge those beliefs?'

Crystallised wisdom: The quiet strength of experience

Psychologist Raymond Cattell distinguished between two kinds of intelligence: *fluid* and *crystallised*.

Fluid intelligence relates to the speed of thinking and problem-solving. It tends to peak earlier in life. Crystallised intelligence, on the other hand, is the accumulated knowledge, insight, and judgement we gain through life experience, and it continues to grow well into later life.

This kind of wisdom matters. It helps us spot patterns, communicate with nuance, and make sound decisions under pressure. In the workplace, it translates into mentoring, leadership, conflict resolution, and big-picture thinking.

Too often, older adults internalise the myth that they are in decline. But recognising crystallised wisdom can help reframe that story and restore a sense of quiet confidence in what they still offer.

Naming the layers of ageism

Some clients have been sidelined directly: overlooked in meetings, left off emails, passed over with vague explanations. Others describe more subtle slights, silence, jokes, or being spoken to as if fragile or fading.

Naming these experiences can be validating. It doesn't create victimhood; it creates clarity. Useful questions include:

- 'What's been said, or left unsaid, that made you feel "othered"?'
- 'Was there a moment when you felt quietly underestimated, and why did it stay with you?'

Naming helps clients understand that these experiences are real, but not the whole story.

> ### What it means to be 'othered'
>
> To be *'othered'* means being subtly or overtly treated as different, lesser, or not belonging, especially in ways that reinforce exclusion or power imbalances. It might not be open discrimination; sometimes it's a glance, a silence, a shift in tone, or being consistently left out. These moments can leave a quiet, lingering sense that you're not fully accepted, even when nothing explicit is said.

Holding an intersectional lens

Rarely is age the only factor. Clients may also be navigating ethnicity, class, gender, health, or background-based bias. A 62-year-old White executive and a 62-year-old working-class Black woman do not experience ageism the same way. You may like to ask:

- 'Are there other parts of your identity that shape how you're seen at work?'
- 'Have you ever felt doubly judged for age and something else?'
- 'What shaped your journey into (or back into) work, beyond your age?'

Tip: Listening for the full story, not just the 'older worker' label, is what builds trust and shows respect for the complexity of lived experience.

> An intersectional lens means understanding that people experience discrimination or privilege in overlapping ways, not just because of one identity (like age), but a combination (such as age *and* ethnicity, gender, class, sexuality, or disability).

Reframing internalised ageism: The quiet saboteur

Perhaps the most insidious form of ageism is internal. Clients may say, 'I'm probably too old for that', with a shrug and a smile, but underneath sits resignation. These beliefs can shape posture, voice, and choices, often before any employer has said a word.

As coaches, we're invited to listen for what's being said and what's being limited.

Rather than offering false reassurance, we create space to explore where those beliefs came from, and what still feels true.

Many midlife and later-life workers have internalised ageist assumptions about decline, redundancy, or diminished value that mirror the messages embedded in workplace culture. Coaching can help name and challenge these beliefs, opening space for renewed agency and possibility.

For many workers over 60, the workplace can feel like a crossroads, uncertain and under-supported. With the right coaching, this pivot point can become a site of reinvention rather than retreat.

Gentle prompts can open the door:

- 'Where did that belief come from?'
- 'What are you still learning, even now?'
- 'If you spoke to yourself with the kindness that you offer others, what would you say about your value?'

Reframing doesn't mean pretending everything is possible. It means helping clients reclaim what is, and recognise the quiet ways they've already resisted the script.

Reframing identity and value

One of the most empowering coaching roles in later-life career support is helping clients tell a stronger story about who they are and what they offer. This section focuses on how to help clients reframe their identity, language, and self-presentation so that they project confidence, value, and contemporary relevance, without trying to hide their age.

Clients often arrive with a belief that they must either apologise for their age or conceal it. Career coaching here becomes about repositioning expertise as a strength and reframing the narrative in a way that aligns with modern workplace needs.

From 'past experience' to 'present value'

Clients may speak in a retrospective tone:

> 'I used to lead teams . . .'
> 'I once managed major projects . . .'
> 'Back in the day . . .'

While their experience is significant, the challenge is to help them translate past achievements into present relevance.

Coaching techniques:

As coaches, we can use *skills translation* tools to identify current-day applications of historic roles. We can reframe examples using *problem–solution–result* language. We can also practise narrative transitions like:

> 'What that means for organisations today is . . .'
> 'Here's how I still apply that skill in current contexts . . .'

As we work with clients, we encourage them to stay in the present tense. Employers want to know not just what someone *has done*, but what they *can do now*.

What can help:

Skills translation tools, e.g. tools 3.2 and 6.2, help clients reframe and repurpose their experience, turning past roles and achievements into present-day, relevant capabilities. In practice, this might include:

A **worksheet** that asks: 'What did you do? What skill did that require? Where is that skill needed today?'

Exercises that shift language from 'I managed teams in 1998' to 'I bring long-term team leadership experience, including conflict resolution and onboarding systems'.

Claiming adaptability and curiosity

One of the most common myths about older workers is that they're resistant to change or technology. Clients may unconsciously reinforce this by making throwaway comments such as, 'I'm not very techy' or 'I'm old school'.

Rather than countering the stereotype with denial, help clients build a more compelling message around adaptability and a learning mindset.

Coaching strategies:

As coaches, we can explore learning narratives: What have they learned recently? What tech or tools have they adapted to? We can invite storytelling about resilience, pivots, or professional reinventions. We can also help them name curiosity as a core strength. For example:

> I've always been someone who learns through doing; recently I've been teaching myself how to use ChatGPT to stay current.

I recommend that we avoid encouraging clients to *oversell youthfulness*. It's more powerful to own experience while showing growth.

In an era of constant disruption, it's not just adaptability that organisations need; it's perspective. Older workers bring what one writer calls the 'momentum of experience': the ability to lead through uncertainty, connect past lessons with emerging challenges, and steady teams in turbulent times. Their insight isn't a relic of the past; it's a vital force for resilience and innovation. When we combine the wisdom of experience with fresh thinking, we create the conditions where intergenerational collaboration truly thrives.

Addressing age with confidence, not caution

Some clients worry they will be 'found out' for being older. This fear can lead to a defensive tone in interviews or applications, such as over-explaining career breaks or apologising for experience. A better approach is to own one's stage of life while emphasising value, perspective, and continuity.

For example:

> Instead of: 'Although I've been out of work for a while . . .'
> Try: 'Over the past year, I've been supporting my family and now bring fresh energy and commitment to the next phase of my work.'

Or:

> Instead of: 'I know I might be older than some applicants . . .'
> Try: 'With deep experience in this area, I bring stability, perspective, and a collaborative mindset; I work well across all generations.'

Coaching clients to rehearse these responses with a neutral tone and clarity helps reduce self-sabotage and enhances credibility.

Refreshing language and LinkedIn presence

Online presence is often where age bias begins, not because of age itself, but because of dated language, formatting, or tone. We can encourage clients to use clear, contemporary language (not heavy jargon or overly formal phrasing), to update job titles and descriptions to align with today's terminology. If not formally employed, we can get them to highlight *current engagement,* such as volunteering, learning, mentoring. And on LinkedIn, they should include a strong, concise headline focused on skills and impact, not chronology. See Chapter 3 for more information.

Clients don't need to deny their age, but they do need to signal relevance, readiness, and vitality.

Coaching prompts: Repositioning and reframing in later life

You won't be using all of these questions; choose a few to ask a client or provide this as a handout to form a discussion in a subsequent session.

Self-reflection

- 'How do you talk about your experience: as something behind you, or something you still use today?'
- 'What story do you want people to hear when they first meet you?'
- 'What do you believe about being your age in the workplace? Where did that belief come from?'

Skills translation

- 'Which parts of your experience still feel alive, useful, or energising?'
- 'What problems have you solved that still matter today, and how?'
- 'If you had to rewrite your experience in today's language, how would it sound?'

Rehearsing confidence

- 'What's one line you can use to express your value without apology?'
- 'How can you describe your adaptability without downplaying your experience?'
- 'If a younger colleague asked what makes you a strong collaborator, what would you say?'

Presence and visibility

- 'What does "contemporary" mean to you, and how do you express that in your tone, your CV, and on LinkedIn?'
- 'How would you like to be seen in this next phase of your working life?'
- 'Where do you already feel current, curious, or connected; and how can you build on that?'

Adapting to the new world of work

Staying yourself in a shifting landscape
Work has changed, not just in tools, but in tempo, tone, and expectations. For clients in midlife and beyond, it's not just about keeping up with technology; it's about finding ways to adapt without losing themselves in the process.

The familiar structures of traditional workplaces – clear hierarchies, formal communication, and long-term planning – have given way to agile teams, rapid feedback cycles, and platforms that most clients in their 50s and 60s never encountered in their early careers. Remote work, collaboration apps, and informal communication norms can feel jarring, not because clients are incapable, but because the landscape has shifted dramatically without them.

As one client in her late 50s said, 'It's not that I don't want to learn, I just feel like everyone's speaking a language I wasn't taught.'

Reframing the challenge
This isn't about 'getting with the times' or proving you can still compete. It's about adapting in ways that feel authentic and sustainable. Clients don't need to master every tool or mimic younger colleagues, but they do need to feel they have a place, a voice, and something valuable to offer.

Coaching in this space begins by validating the learning curve. 'It's not you, it's a new context', we might say. Digital fluency isn't about mastery; it's about the willingness to ask, explore, and adapt in unfamiliar environments.

From confidence gaps to competence gaps
Often, what looks like a technical problem is really a confidence wobble. Clients may feel anxious about looking slow or outdated, and that anxiety can block learning. Helping them separate what they *don't know* from what they *assume they can't learn* is a key early step. A short tutorial or guided practice can shift mindset more than a formal course.

Work culture is changing too
Adapting also means understanding how work cultures have evolved. Informality, experimentation, and flatter structures can be energising or alienating, depending on your experience. For some, being addressed by their first name in an email from a CEO is refreshing; for others, it's unsettling.

Many clients hold internalised beliefs about what's 'professional', what's 'respectful', and how authority works. Coaching can gently explore these assumptions without judgement. What's useful to hold onto, and what might be ready to loosen?

- 'Which parts of this new work culture feel energising?'
- 'Where do you already have strengths that could thrive in this kind of environment?'

Adapting without erasing

Adaptability in later life isn't about starting over; it's about bringing who you are into new formats. That might mean:

- Contributing legacy wisdom to younger, agile teams.
- Participating in co-creation rather than top-down planning.
- Embracing 'just-in-time' learning rather than long-term mastery.
- Remaining open to role redefinition mid-project or mid-contract.

We can ask:

- 'In what ways have you already adapted in life or work, even if you didn't label it that way?'
- 'What would it mean to be digitally confident, not digitally perfect?'

When clients start to see themselves not as obsolete but as evolving, the energy shifts. They stop asking, 'Do I still belong here?' and start asking, 'How can I belong in a way that works for me now?'

Working across generations

Connection, not competition

Modern workplaces are often multigenerational; five generations, in some cases, working side by side. For clients in midlife and later life, this can offer enormous potential for shared learning and layered perspectives. But it can also bring tension: between values, communication styles, expectations, and unspoken assumptions about who belongs where.

Some clients find themselves reporting to managers 20 or 30 years younger. Others feel invisible in meetings, unsure how to contribute without sounding patronising or outdated. The discomfort may not be voiced, but it's felt.

One client, a 63-year-old with decades of leadership experience, described it like this: 'I feel like an old oak tree in a room full of saplings. I'm sturdy, I have roots, but I'm not sure anyone sees my relevance anymore.'

As coaches, our role is not to 'fix' this dynamic, but to help clients navigate it with awareness, generosity, and confidence.

Understanding generational mindsets
Each generation is shaped by its own cultural, historical, and technological context. These differences show up in how people approach:

- work–life balance;
- authority and leadership;
- communication (email versus Slack, formal versus informal);
- career loyalty and pace of change.

Misunderstandings can arise quickly: older clients may see younger colleagues as impatient or lacking depth. Younger workers may see older team members as resistant or slow to adapt. Miscommunications escalate when filtered through bias, stress, or unfamiliar norms. But behind the friction are shared human needs, to be respected, heard, and valued.

Coaching can help clients gently reflect on their own assumptions:

- 'What stories are you carrying about other generations?'
- 'What reactions in you might be less about them, and more about old patterns?'

Understanding doesn't mean agreement. But it can soften the edge enough to start a new kind of conversation.

From relevance to rapport
Fear of being seen as irrelevant is common and understandable. Some clients respond by withdrawing, others by overcompensating: overusing jargon, joking about their age, or pushing to prove they're 'still sharp'. But relevance isn't about mimicry; it's about resonance.

Help clients reconnect with the value they offer: perspective, context, calm in a crisis. These qualities are not dated but a solid foundation.

Invite them to consider:

- 'How can I show up as a guide or partner, not a competitor?'
- 'Where might curiosity be more useful than comparison?'

Clients who lead with presence, who ask questions, share stories appropriately, and listen well, often find that connection begins to build.

When the manager is younger
This is one of the most emotionally charged dynamics in later-life coaching. A client might say, 'They're younger than my son! How can I take direction from them?'

The discomfort is real, and it often touches deeper questions of status, identity, and self-worth. Normalising this unease is an important first step. But it's equally important to explore the other side: What is this younger manager navigating? What pressures are they under? What could your client offer that supports rather than threatens?

One shift that helps is to support your client to move from 'how do I protect my authority?' to 'how do I build trust?' Help them to understand that trust doesn't mean deference; it means reliability, mutual respect, and openness to collaboration.

This framing helps clients stay grounded:

- 'How can I support them to succeed without giving up my own voice?'
- 'What does respectful assertiveness look like in this relationship?'

OLEKSANDR, 61: FINDING COMMON GROUND WITH A YOUNGER MANAGER

Oleksandr, a programme manager, had recently joined a sustainability consultancy led by a much younger leadership team. His new line manager, Zoe, was 31. 'She's sharp and capable', he said, 'but I keep second-guessing how to speak up. I don't want to come across as patronising or out of touch.'

In coaching, Oleksandr admitted he felt unsure of his role. 'I've spent years mentoring others, and now I'm holding back. I'm worried I'll sound like someone's dad.'

We explored what leadership looks like in intergenerational teams, and how he might move from a directive stance to a collaborative presence. He reframed his value: not as a senior authority, but as a stabiliser, someone who could ask thoughtful questions, build bridges across teams, and offer historical insight without needing the spotlight.

Later, he shared a moment when Zoe thanked him for a quiet suggestion that helped defuse a tense client meeting. 'I realised I didn't need to prove myself. I just needed to be available, open, and steady.'

Coaching reflection:

- Some clients need help shifting from *status* to *stewardship;* from leading through authority to leading through presence.
- Fear of being patronising or irrelevant can create withdrawal. Reframing their role as a guide or collaborator can restore confidence.

Coaching questions might include:

- 'What kind of support can you offer without stepping over the line?'
- 'Where can you bring quiet leadership, through listening, steadiness, or insight?'

Mutual learning, not one-way teaching

Reverse mentoring, where younger colleagues share digital or cultural insights, is gaining traction. It doesn't need to be formal. Many older clients light up when they realise they're still learning and contributing, just in a different rhythm.

Encourage clients to see mentoring as a two-way process and to share their wisdom without assuming it's always needed. They can be moved to receive feedback or insight from younger colleagues as an invitation, not a threat.

One client in his late 50s put it this way: 'I stopped trying to be impressive, and just started being available. And suddenly, people wanted to hear what I had to say.' That's the shift: from proving worth to offering value. From holding ground to opening doors.

Accommodations and health-supportive strategies

Working well with the body and mind you have now

As people live and work longer, it's increasingly common to navigate health conditions, changing energy levels, or fluctuating capacity while still wanting to contribute meaningfully. Yet many clients in midlife or later life hesitate to ask for support. They may worry about being labelled as 'less capable' or fear becoming a burden.

The result? They overextend, stay silent, or quietly step back, not because they can't work, but because the way they've always worked no longer fits.

Coaching in this situation isn't about managing illness. It's about helping clients design sustainable ways of working that align with who they are now, not who they were ten years ago.

Changing health, changing energy

Clients often arrive with quiet frustration or grief about their shifting capacity. 'I used to run teams and pull late nights', one said. 'Now three back-to-back meetings wipe me out.' The change can feel disorienting, not just physically, but in terms of identity.

The coaching task is to create space for that grief, then gently pivot towards acceptance and adaptation. This might include:

- exploring pacing and realistic work rhythms;
- identifying energy drainers versus energy givers; and
- using practical tools like energy budgeting or priority mapping.

It helps to normalise the shift, and we can say something like: 'Your capacity may have changed. Your value hasn't.'

Knowing your rights, without shame

Many clients don't realise they're entitled to support. Depending on the country, this might include:

- reasonable accommodations or adjustments;
- flexible working arrangements; and
- legal protection against discrimination.

But information alone isn't enough. Clients often need language and confidence to express what they need. That's where coaching plays a vital role, not in giving legal advice, but in helping clients:

- role-play conversations with employers or HR;
- frame requests as enabling performance, not seeking favours; and
- focus on outcomes, not diagnoses.

For example, rather than disclosing an entire medical history, a client might simply say, 'To do my best work, I need a quieter space in the afternoon, and a 10-minute reset break mid-morning'.

Disclosure is a choice, not a requirement

One of the most delicate questions clients face is: *'Do I tell my employer about my condition?'* There's no single answer, only what feels safe and useful. Some clients want to be open but don't know how. Others fear stigma or being sidelined.

Coaching here is about agency and clarity. Instead of 'Should I disclose?', you might explore:

- 'What do you want them to know, and why?'
- 'What's the outcome you're hoping for?'
- 'How can you explain your needs without oversharing your experience?'

The goal is a simple, strong narrative. Not a full disclosure, but a clear boundary: 'This is what I need to work well.'

Rethinking what 'good work' looks like

Sometimes, the shift isn't only about health; it's about recognising that the way we work in later life **can** and **should** evolve. For some clients, this means:

- Moving into portfolio or part-time roles.
- Shifting towards less cognitively or physically demanding tasks.
- Building in space between commitments for recovery.
- Exploring meaningful unpaid or low-pressure work.

This isn't giving up. It's growing wiser. Coaching can help reframe success, not as doing it all, but doing what matters, in a way that sustains wellbeing over time. One client put it beautifully: 'I used to aim for productivity. Now I aim for presence.'

Rethinking employability in later life

Redefining what it means to be hireable in later life

The word *employability* often conjures images of youth, career climbing, and long-term ambition. But in today's work landscape, shaped by skill shortages, project-based hiring, and a growing emphasis on values and fit, those old associations are breaking down.

For clients in midlife and beyond, the challenge isn't to 'compete with younger workers', but to understand and articulate their evolving value in ways that feel relevant and real.

What employability looks like now

In your 50s, 60s, or 70s, employability isn't mainly about being at the top of your game; it's about being game: willing to learn, contribute, adapt, and engage. It might show up as:

- emotional steadiness in uncertain environments;
- the ability to navigate ambiguity and offer perspective;
- a collaborative spirit grounded in experience;
- curiosity, not complacency; and
- a clear, credible skill set (even if it's narrower or deeper than before).

Coaching clients to focus on what they offer *now*, rather than what they used to be, is key: 'What do you bring that a team needs right now, not just over the next 10 years?'

This shift can be liberating. It's no longer about longevity. It's about fit and value in the present.

Reclaiming visibility

Many older clients are quietly competent and quietly invisible. They may resist social media or an online presence. They downplay new training or recent achievements, assuming they're too small to matter. Some feel unsure how to describe who they are now, especially if they're in transition.

Coaching can help them find a voice that's clear but not boastful. A few practical moves can make a big difference:

- Refreshing LinkedIn with current language and present-tense framing.
- Writing a short, confident introduction that doesn't apologise for age or gaps.
- Speaking up in meetings, not with dominance, but with a grounded presence.

The aim isn't noise. It's signal. 'I'm still here, and I still have something to offer.'

Longevity in the 50s: Building forward

Clients in their 50s often want to keep working for another 10–15 years, but feel unsure how to stay relevant without burning out. Many have responsibilities at both ends: teens at home, parents needing support, and they are tired of proving themselves.

Here, coaching focuses on sustainability, not last-ditch reinvention:

- What do you want to be known for?
- What skills or knowledge need refreshing?
- Where could you show up more visibly, through mentoring, writing, or speaking?
- What lateral moves or flexible options are available?

Clients don't always need big shifts. Sometimes they need permission to slow the pace and still remain impactful.

Purposeful contribution in the 60s and 70s

For clients in their 60s and 70s, employability often becomes less about income and more about meaning, structure, and self-worth. Some want continued stimulation. Others want community. A few want to give back, without being drained.

Coaching helps them surface what matters now:

- 'What kind of contribution feels most aligned?'
- 'How much structure do you want, and how much freedom?'

- 'Where could your wisdom be welcomed, not just tolerated?'

This might lead to short-term consulting, mentoring, governance roles, or starting something of their own. The format matters less than the fit, the sense that their experience still matters, and that they can shape what comes next on their own terms.

The AI lens on employability

In today's evolving work environment, perceptions of employability are increasingly influenced by technology, especially artificial intelligence. But AI systems, including hiring algorithms and digital platforms, can unintentionally reinforce age bias. Older candidates may be filtered out by proxies such as graduation dates, tech language, or employment gaps. Many tools are designed with younger users in mind, making older workers feel invisible or excluded. Helping clients build digital confidence and frame tech use as a sign of adaptability, not deficiency, can be a powerful way to reclaim relevance and visibility in an AI-shaped world.

Coaching prompts: Reframing tech confidence

Use these questions to support clients who feel uncertain or resistant about technology, especially in the context of ageing, career change, or shifting work demands.

- How do you feel about the role of technology, especially AI, in your current or future work?
- What would help you feel more confident, curious, or engaged with the tools emerging around you?
- Are there small steps you could take, like attending a webinar, experimenting with a new platform, or asking a peer for help, that would allow you to explore without pressure?

Finding the right workplace fit

Finding the right place to contribute

Not all employers are resistant to age. In fact, many are beginning to recognise the value of age-diverse teams, not just for fairness but for strategy. As demographics shift and skills shortages grow, organisations are waking up to the potential of older workers: calm under pressure, seasoned in relationships, rich in insight.

But that recognition isn't yet consistent. Some workplaces are ahead of the curve. Others still see age as a problem to manage rather than an asset to welcome. For clients, the challenge is not only to remain employable but to find environments where they can thrive.

What age-inclusive really looks like

True age inclusion goes beyond avoiding discrimination. It means actively designing for participation across the lifespan. This might include:

- Recruitment practices that welcome older applicants.
- Flexible working options that support changing life rhythms.
- Learning and development opportunities at every age.
- Visible representation of older people in leadership or public-facing roles.
- An explicit appreciation of intergenerational collaboration.

Clients often ask, *'How can I tell if a workplace values someone like me?'*

The signs are there if you know where to look:

- Language in job adverts that avoids coded terms like 'energetic graduate' or 'digital native'.
- Age-diverse imagery and storytelling on company websites.
- Evidence of phased retirement, job sharing, or flexibility by design.
- Older staff speaking at events or profiled in internal communications.
- Age being named explicitly as part of the organisation's Diversity, equity, and inclusion (DEI) strategy.

As coaches, we can help clients tune into these subtle signals and trust their gut when something feels off.

Skills-based hiring and learning cultures

One promising shift is the growing move from credentials to capabilities. More employers are hiring for what people *can do,* not just where they've worked or what degrees they hold. For experienced professionals, this is good news. But it also means reframing experience as capability, not chronology. Clients may need help to translate their past into present relevance. They need to be able to answer well against these three areas:

- Here's how I solve problems.
- This is how I work in a team.
- These are the tools I've learned, and how I'm still learning.

Learning, too, has changed. Clients may benefit from environments that support growth without pressure, from self-paced digital courses to peer-led skill swaps. The key is mindset. It's never about knowing everything. It's about being willing to learn publicly and resisting the whisper that 'I should know this by now'.

Choosing the right culture, not just the right role
Sometimes it's not the job that's wrong, it's the environment. High-pressure, always-on cultures may no longer feel sustainable or meaningful. A client might not need a break from work, but a break from *that kind* of work.

Coaching can open up new questions:

- 'What kind of pace or rhythm suits you now?'
- 'Do you want more structure, or more autonomy?'
- 'Where might your experience be welcomed, not simply tolerated?'

Clients may find they're better matched to smaller firms, social enterprises, public sector roles, or purpose-led start-ups. The goal isn't to lower ambition; it's to realign ambition with identity.

Encourage clients to assess employers not just by title or salary, but by tone; the ecosystem, the energy, and the values on display.

Advocating for change, when you can
While most coaching stays client-centred, some clients, or coaches, will feel called to shape broader change. They may be in HR roles, management, or informal leadership positions. They may want to speak up.

That might look like:

- Offering insights to improve age inclusion in hiring.
- Challenging assumptions around training, visibility, or digital comfort.
- Encouraging peer-to-peer mentoring across generations.
- Modelling respectful, age-diverse teamwork in their own practice.

Even small acts, a comment in a meeting, a profile in a newsletter, can challenge the narrative that age equals decline.

We can support clients to find their voice in this space if they choose to use it, not out of defensiveness but as part of creating the kind of workplaces they'd want to join.

Closing reflections

Reclaiming relevance in a changing world
Coaching clients through age-related workplace dynamics isn't about protecting them from change. It's about helping them move through it, with clarity, dignity, and a renewed sense of personal power.

Some will arrive angry. Others ashamed, cautious, or quietly uncertain about whether they still belong. Many carry a history of being overlooked, misunderstood, or underused. And yet, they also bring something rare: perspective, steadiness, patience, and lived wisdom that doesn't come from a course or a CV.

In a fast-moving work culture, clients don't need to become faster. They need to become clearer about what they offer, what matters, and what they want from this chapter. Whether they're navigating bias, adapting to new tech, or negotiating boundaries shaped by health or caregiving, your role is to hold the space for courage and possibility.

Change may be constant, but so is the right to belong, contribute, and be valued at every age.

For further evidence on employer attitudes and structural barriers, see the CIPD's 2022 report, *Understanding Older Workers*.

In a nutshell

- Ageism can be overt or subtle, and often intersects with gender, ethnicity, class, and health.
- Later-life clients may question their relevance, but they bring perspective, stability, and insight.
- Adapting to modern work doesn't mean becoming someone else; it means integrating old strengths with new tools.
- Intergenerational teams thrive when clients relate with curiosity, not comparison.
- Health changes require honest reflection, boundary-setting, and confidence in self-advocacy.
- Employability isn't about age; it's about readiness, value, and contribution.
- The best-fit workplaces are those where clients feel respected, not just hired.
- Coaching can support both personal agency and cultural change, one conversation at a time.
- Our job isn't to help clients fight ageism alone; it's to walk beside them as they reclaim their place, their presence, and their evolving story at work.

Chapter 9
Portfolio careers, self-employment, encore careers, and unretirement

> **Summary**
>
> *In later life, work often becomes less about climbing and more about crafting. This chapter explores four evolving patterns: portfolio careers, self-employment, encore careers, and unretirement, and how they offer freedom, purpose, and rhythm beyond traditional employment. It provides coaching strategies, emotional insight, and practical tools to help clients navigate these paths with clarity and confidence.*

Redefining work in later life

Many later-life career journeys do not follow a single, linear path. They emerge through exploration, curiosity, or even chance, as seen in stories of individuals who pivot from law to chocolate-making, academia to life design, or medical careers to fine art. These stories remind us that second acts are not a fallback. They are often the first time someone truly aligns their work with joy, contribution, and autonomy.

The traditional model of retirement – a hard stop followed by permanent leisure – no longer fits the lives, needs, or aspirations of many people in their 50s, 60s, and beyond. And for some in midlife, it's not retirement at all that's on the horizon, but a desire to reshape work now, before it becomes unsustainable or misaligned. Increasingly, clients are seeking a more flexible, meaningful, and self-directed relationship with work. They're not necessarily chasing promotion or full-time roles, but they're not ready to 'retire' either.

Some want to stay engaged but with more freedom. Others want to change direction, try something new, or finally pursue long-held dreams. A growing number of clients want to create their own work, combining income with autonomy and purpose.

This chapter explores four overlapping later-life patterns:

- **Portfolio careers**: A blend of roles, income streams, and professional identities.
- **Self-employment**: From consultancy and freelancing to purpose-led projects or businesses.
- **Encore careers**: Purpose-driven roles in later life that blend income with social impact, often emerging from a desire to give back or leave a legacy.
- **Unretirement**: The conscious choice to return to work after a period of retirement.

Each of these paths reflects a desire for agency, rhythm, and relevance. As coaches, we can support clients in navigating these non-traditional choices, balancing realism with optimism, and structure with experimentation.

Portfolio careers: Designing a richer tapestry of work and life

For many in midlife and beyond, the idea of a single job, even a single identity, starts to feel limiting. A portfolio career offers a richer alternative: a way to bring together multiple strands of work, income, and meaning. Rather than a linear path, it's a more mosaic approach, with part-time roles, freelance work, mentoring, volunteering, or creative pursuits woven into a rhythm that suits the person they are now.

This shift is often less about ambition and more about alignment. Clients come to coaching looking not just for the next role, but for a sustainable way of working that reflects who they are becoming. For some, it's about staying connected to their professional roots, consulting in a familiar sector or mentoring others, while also making space for long-suppressed passions. For others, it's about building something entirely new.

Take, for example, my own evolving career. After years as a psychologist, author, and career coach, I've found that a portfolio life allows me to keep doing meaningful work, but on my own terms. I still offer coaching and consultancy, but I've also shifted into more reflective, purpose-led activities: writing books, facilitating nature retreats, and guiding wilderness rites of passage. I even own a small woodland, which has become a backdrop for some of this work, a place where reflection and reconnection take root and where I've built a deeper connection with nature, enjoying the physical aspects of woodland management. These varied roles aren't just practical; they express different aspects of who I am and what I care about.

Clients who explore a portfolio life often describe it as liberating, but not without challenges. There's a need to manage boundaries, structure time wisely, and make peace with ambiguity. Some worry they'll look unfocused or feel unsure about how to present themselves professionally when they 'do a bit of everything'. Part of our role as coaches is to help them surface the coherence that lies beneath the variety. What values link these roles? What themes or threads run through their work and life?

It's also important to attend to energy and capacity. We can help clients map their energy across the week or month, ensuring they don't overload themselves in the early enthusiasm of reinvention. This is about building a rhythm, not just a schedule, that supports health, meaning, and joy.

Portfolio clients may struggle with traditional notions of success. They might not be chasing promotion or a clear job title anymore. But they are pursuing something more enduring: a life of engagement, flexibility, contribution, and personal resonance.

Coaching questions can help open up this space. Instead of asking 'What job do you want?' we might ask, 'What would your ideal week include?' or 'Which parts of you have been waiting to emerge?' We can also explore identity: 'What would it take to feel confident introducing yourself with more than one hat?' or 'Which role in your portfolio feels most aligned with who you are now?'

A portfolio career isn't just a workaround; it's a design for living. And for many in later life, it's not a compromise; it's a liberation.

ANITA, 63: BRIDGING ROLES, REDEFINING SELF

Anita came to coaching after leaving a senior leadership role in education. 'I thought I'd relish the freedom', she said, 'but I missed having a reason to get up in the morning'. She wasn't interested in full-time work again, but retirement didn't feel like a fit either. 'I have more to give; I just don't want it to take over my life.'

Through coaching, Anita began to explore what she called her 'career fragments': mentoring young teachers, facilitating diversity workshops, and writing short stories she'd long kept in a drawer. Rather than choose one path, she started to blend them. Two days a week, she consulted for a charity focused on educational access. One day, she offered mentoring sessions. The rest of the week, she protected time for her creative writing and joined a local storytelling group.

'I used to introduce myself as a headteacher. Now I say I'm a writer, a mentor, and an educator-at-large. It took me a while to believe all those things could belong together.' 'It's not retirement', she smiled, 'it's realignment'.

The portfolio gave her not just variety, but rhythm and meaning. She learned to manage her energy, set clearer boundaries, and embrace her evolving identity.

Coaching reflection: Later-life transitions aren't always about choosing one path; they're about integrating what feels meaningful now. Coaching can help clients embrace a portfolio identity with confidence and clarity.

RAVI, 53: REFOCUSING BEFORE BURNOUT

Ravi had worked in marketing for over 25 years, most recently as a senior strategist for a global brand. He wasn't unhappy, but he was starting to feel detached. 'I kept thinking, this isn't bad . . . but is this how I want to spend the next ten years?' he said. The pace was relentless, and his sense of contribution had faded.

Coaching gave Ravi permission to explore a change before reaching crisis point. He described himself as 'not ready to retire, but ready to recalibrate'. Together, we mapped his values, energy rhythms, and interests outside the corporate world. He'd always loved mentoring younger professionals and had a long-standing interest in ethical food systems.

Within six months, Ravi negotiated a three-day consultancy retainer with his former employer, began mentoring through a start-up incubator, and joined a local social enterprise supporting sustainable agriculture. His work life became more diverse and aligned.

'I didn't want to blow it all up', he reflected. 'I just wanted to feel like I was living with intention again.'

Coaching reflection: Coaching can offer space to recalibrate before a crisis. Small shifts, guided by values and energy, can bring renewed purpose without abandoning hard-earned expertise.

MARIA, 67: FINANCIAL NEED, CREATIVE RESPONSE

Maria hadn't planned to work after retirement. But rising living costs and supporting her adult daughter pushed her to rethink. 'I didn't want to go back to retail full-time, but I needed something', she said.

Coaching helped her map her skills: customer service, crafting, event organising, and experimenting with options. She took a part-time admin role at a local arts centre and started selling handmade jewellery at weekend markets. Through a connection, she began coordinating seasonal fairs, leading to more freelance event work.

'At first, I felt embarrassed, like I'd failed at retirement', Maria admitted. 'But now I see I've created something I enjoy. It's not what I expected, but it's mine.'

Her portfolio career was born not just from choice but from necessity, giving her agency, activity, and autonomy.

Coaching reflection: Necessity can be a powerful catalyst. Coaching helps clients like Maria respond creatively, blending income needs with agency, enjoyment, and evolving self-definition.

DEREK, 58: FROM CORPORATE TO CREATIVE BLEND

Derek had spent over three decades in financial services, most recently as a regional manager. After a redundancy package and a period of burnout, he knew he didn't want to return to the same environment. 'I'd lost track of what I enjoyed; everything became about performance targets.'

Coaching helped him reconnect with earlier interests: public speaking, mentoring younger colleagues, and restoring vintage motorbikes. He began giving talks on financial literacy to community groups, took on part-time consulting work with SMEs, and started restoring bikes, eventually selling a few for profit.

'I used to think I needed a job title to feel legitimate', he reflected. 'Now I think in terms of contribution and flow. Each strand feeds a different part of me.'

His week now blends consulting, community work, and hands-on craft. His income is lower, but his satisfaction is much higher.

Coaching reflection: Portfolio careers can emerge from burnout as much as ambition. Coaching supports clients in designing work that reflects their values, energy, and broader sense of contribution.

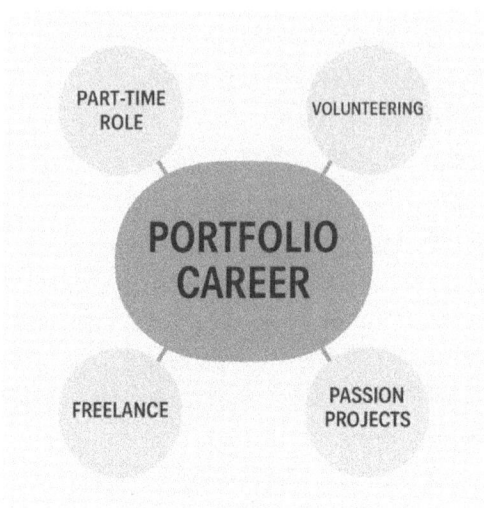

Portfolio careers: A design for living

Portfolio careers in later life aren't just a way to keep working; they're a way to keep becoming. Clients often seek not a single role but a rhythm: one that allows space for meaning, energy management, and multiple identities. Coaching can help them integrate their skills, passions, and commitments into a life that feels coherent and self-defined. This isn't a fallback; it's a liberation.

Late bloomers in business: Why 50+ entrepreneurs often thrive

Starting a business in your 50s or 60s might seem risky, but the data tells a different story. Research consistently shows that older entrepreneurs are more likely to succeed than their younger counterparts. They bring deep sector knowledge, mature networks, financial stability, and realistic expectations. In fact, one UK study found that start-ups led by over-50s are more likely to still be trading after five years than those led by under-30s.

Some launch a business out of choice, to pursue a passion or create an impact. Others do so out of necessity, after redundancy or age-related barriers in traditional employment. And many combine income generation with lifestyle design, autonomy, or flexible contribution.

Stepping into self-employment: Freedom with purpose

While portfolio careers often involve a blend of multiple activities across domains, self-employment focuses more specifically on creating income independently. This could mean consulting in a former field, turning a creative interest into a business, or launching something new in a sector aligned with personal values.

For many clients in midlife and beyond, self-employment is not just an economic shift; it's a mindset change. It reflects a desire for more autonomy, purpose, and rhythm, often emerging from a need to leave behind the structures that no longer fit.

Self-employment takes many forms in later life: consulting in a familiar field, turning a creative interest into a small business, launching a community-led venture, or freelancing across several domains. What links these pathways is not just the work itself, but the mindset shift, from jobholder to value giver, from employee to creative contributor.

Some clients step in confidently, excited by the possibilities. Others feel daunted. The freedom appeals, but so does the structure of a steady job. Many wrestle with the fear of 'selling themselves', managing finances, or navigating technology.

For some, the idea of visibility feels uncomfortable. They imagine self-employment requires relentless promotion or polished branding. But visibility in later life can be gentle. It can grow through contribution, through showing up, offering value, and letting word of mouth do its quiet work. We can help clients reframe visibility not as self-promotion but as service.

As coaches, we help clients begin from where they are. We don't need to be business experts; our job is to help them clarify their values, test small ideas, and explore the identity shifts that come with becoming self-employed. It's not about building an empire; it's about building a life that fits.

RAJ, 62: FROM POSSIBILITY TO PRACTICE

Raj took voluntary redundancy after a long career in logistics. He didn't want to stop working, but returning to a rigid corporate structure held no appeal. At first, the idea of self-employment felt overwhelming. He wasn't interested in branding or building a website. But in coaching, he reframed the challenge: he didn't need to 'market' himself; he just needed to reconnect with three trusted colleagues and offer practical help with clear value. Within a few months, Raj was working two days a week with two small firms, selecting projects that matched his expertise and keeping his freedom intact. His self-employment wasn't about reinvention; it was about alignment.

YVONNE, 58: TURNING PASSION INTO A GENTLE VENTURE

Yvonne had a part-time job in finance and a passion for making natural skincare products. Friends regularly requested her creams and balms, but she'd never thought of turning it into more than a hobby. Coaching helped her explore that question: what would 'more' look like, and what didn't she want it to become?

She started small, selling a trial batch at a local market. When it sold out, she launched a modest online shop, balancing her creative outlet with her existing role. For Yvonne, success wasn't about scaling up; it was about joy, connection, and expressing a different part of herself.

CLAIRE, 64: NAVIGATING SELF-EMPLOYMENT WITH HEALTH LIMITATIONS

Claire had worked as a marketing manager until a chronic fatigue condition made full-time employment unsustainable. 'I still have so much to give', she said, 'but I can't push through like I used to'.

In coaching, she explored consultancy work that offered both flexibility and autonomy. We focused on pacing, rest rhythms, and protecting her energy while maintaining her confidence.

Claire now takes on small, high-value copywriting projects with long deadlines. She also co-hosts a peer support group for women navigating health changes and later-life transitions. 'Self-employment gives me choice', she said. 'But it only works because I respect my limits.'

DANIEL, 67: FINDING PURPOSE AFTER RETIREMENT

Daniel had officially retired from teaching, but found himself restless and unfulfilled. 'I didn't realise how much I'd miss being useful', he said. In coaching, he revisited a long-standing love of stories and community education. He began running small life-story workshops at local centres and care homes.

Though unpaid at first, word of mouth led to speaking opportunities and paid work with a hospice charity. Registering as self-employed helped him manage his earnings and give his work a clear structure, but the deeper motivation was always purpose. For Daniel, it wasn't about building a business. It was about continuing to matter.

COACHING TOOL 9.1: Is self-employment right for me?

A reflective tool for exploring readiness and alignment

This tool helps clients explore whether self-employment is a meaningful and viable path: emotionally, practically, and personally. It can be used in coaching conversations, as a journalling guide, or as a workshop handout.

1. **Motivation**
   - What's drawing you towards self-employment at this stage?
   - Are you motivated by freedom, purpose, income, creativity, or something else?
   - Beyond money, what does success look like to you?
2. **Confidence check**
   - What part of this excites you?
   - What part feels intimidating or unfamiliar?
   - What do you already know how to do, and where might you need support?
3. **Boundaries and rhythm**
   - How much time and energy do you want to dedicate to this?
   - What kind of weekly or monthly pattern would feel healthy and sustainable?
   - What boundaries would help protect your wellbeing?
4. **Support and connection**
   - Who do you know who's self-employed, and what could you learn from them?
   - What kind of community or peer support would help you stay motivated?
   - Are there local or online groups you could explore?
5. **Small first steps**
   - What's the smallest possible way you could test this idea?
   - What would feel like a meaningful first action, without overcommitting?
   - How will you check in with yourself to review how it's going?

Coaching insight: Supporting clients in the self-employment space

Self-employment requires more than skill; it takes courage, resilience, and a tolerance for ambiguity. As coaches, we can:
- Encourage experimentation before large investments.
- Reframe visibility as value-sharing, not self-promotion.
- Help define 'enough' in time, income, and energy.
- Support mindset shifts: from employee to experimenter, provider to purpose-seeker.

Self-employment: Freedom, gently held

Self-employment in later life is rarely about hustle or growth. More often, it's about reclaiming agency, working in rhythm with energy and health, and aligning contribution with values. Clients may begin with hesitation, but with support, they often discover that self-employment is less about selling themselves and more about showing up with value. It becomes not a performance, but a practice.

Encore careers: Purpose-driven work in later life

For some people in midlife and beyond, the next chapter of work is not about easing into retirement, nor launching a new business, but finding a deeper sense of purpose. Encore careers, a term popularised by Marc Freedman, describe later-life roles that combine income, meaning, and social contribution. These roles often focus on sectors like education, healthcare, the environment, or social justice, where lived experience can be an asset rather than a liability.

Encore careers are not a formal pathway or job title; they are a mindset. Individuals pursuing them are often motivated by the desire to give back, make a difference, or leave a legacy. The work may be paid or low-paid, part-time or flexible, and often emerges from a sense of calling rather than a need to stay employed. For those who have had financially secure careers or taken early retirement, the encore phase can be a deliberate return, not to the old pace, but to a new purpose.

These roles may involve retraining, but not always. Often, it's about repurposing existing skills in a different context, like a former business leader mentoring young entrepreneurs or a project manager moving into the charity sector. Some people pursue encore careers through portfolio work, combining short-term contracts, consulting, or project roles. Others embed them within voluntary or trustee positions that slowly evolve into something more substantial.

From a coaching perspective, it's useful to explore the values, causes, and communities that matter most to clients, as well as the lifestyle and time commitments they want to maintain. Many are not looking for a 'second act' that mirrors the intensity of their former career, but something that offers fulfilment without burnout.

Encore careers often arise from reflection and experimentation, not strategic planning. Clients may need time to explore, prototype, or even 'try on' different roles before something clicks. The question isn't just *What do I want to do next?* but *Who do I want to be in this next phase of life?*

Let's see how things have evolved for David and Lorraine.

DAVID, 62: FROM EARLY RETIREMENT TO PURPOSE-DRIVEN WORK

After a 35-year career in engineering, David took early retirement, planning to relax, travel, and restore his vintage car. But within a year, he felt something was missing. While he didn't want the pressure of full-time work, he missed the sense of purpose and problem-solving that had once energised him.

A chance conversation led him to a local college seeking mentors for STEM students. David began volunteering a few hours a week, helping with project work and offering career advice. The experience rekindled a spark; he realised he still had more to give.

Within six months, he took a part-time role as a technical adviser for a social enterprise refurbishing laptops for disadvantaged families. The work wasn't highly paid, but that wasn't the point. 'I'm using what I know to make things better', he said. 'I finally feel useful again.'

David's encore career wasn't planned; it unfolded through curiosity, conversations, and a willingness to step back in, on his own terms.

LORRAINE, 56: FINDING PURPOSE IN A NEW KIND OF WORK

Lorraine had spent most of her working life in retail, moving from the shop floor to managing a small team. She left during the pandemic, planning a long break. But after two years, the novelty wore off. 'I wasn't ready to stop being useful', she said. 'But I didn't want to go back to the tills.'

Through her local library, Lorraine heard about a part-time support role with a neighbourhood food project. Sorting donations, talking to visitors, and liaising with partners paid modestly, but the real reward was belonging and making a difference.

She later trained as a community food educator, teaching simple, budget-friendly cooking classes. 'I never thought I'd be "teaching" anyone', she laughed. 'But I know how to make a meal from what's in the cupboard.'

Lorraine's encore career didn't involve retraining or climbing a new ladder. It grew from her life experience, values, and community spirit.

Coaching prompt: Exploring encore career possibilities

These prompts support clients in imagining work that feels meaningful, flexible, and aligned with their values in this next life stage. Encore careers are not about climbing again; they're about contributing in ways that matter.

You might ask:

- What causes or issues feel especially meaningful to you at this stage of life?
- Where might your existing skills be valuable beyond your previous career field?
- Are there organisations, communities, or sectors you've long admired or wanted to be part of?
- What balance of income, time, and purpose feels right for you now?
- How might you 'test the waters' through a small project, volunteer role, or short-term contract?
- If you imagined your work as part of your legacy, what would you hope to leave behind?

Encore careers: Returning with purpose

Encore careers are not about starting over. They're about bringing life experience, values, and desire to contribute into focus. Clients may feel drawn to causes or communities, seeking roles where impact matters more than income. Coaching can help them navigate this phase with curiosity, experimentation, prototyping, and finding purpose without pressure. It's not about climbing again; it's about making meaning.

Unretirement: Returning with intention

Not everyone stays retired. For many clients, the reality of retirement doesn't quite match the fantasy. What once promised rest and freedom can, over time, give way to boredom, isolation, or a sense of lost identity. Others step away from work too early, nudged by restructuring, caregiving demands, or assumptions about age, only to realise they still want to contribute.

Unretirement is the conscious decision to return to work after a period of retirement. Sometimes it's driven by financial necessity, but often the reasons run deeper: a desire for connection, stimulation, or purpose. As coaches, we can help clients reflect on what's drawing them back, explore options that suit their current rhythm and energy, and reframe the decision as a meaningful evolution rather than a step backward.

For some, returning is not a choice

While many later-life clients want to continue working for meaning and connection, others feel compelled to do so due to financial necessity. One quick example: if someone needs £35,000 a year to live comfortably but only receives £12,000 from the state pension, they may face a significant shortfall, prompting continued work out of necessity, not choice.

This highlights the importance of coaching conversations that balance **autonomy, energy, and financial realities**, without defaulting to assumptions that everyone can simply 'choose' to retire or work.

Here are some stories of people who have unretired.

ELAINE, 66: REDISCOVERING STRUCTURE AND PURPOSE

Elaine had retired after a long and successful career as a secondary school headteacher. She initially embraced the freedom, spending time in the garden, travelling, and reconnecting with friends, but after a year, a kind of quiet unease settled in. 'I missed the challenge', she admitted. 'And the sense of being part of something bigger.' Coaching helped Elaine explore her options, and she gradually returned to the education world on her own terms, mentoring new teachers and doing occasional cover work at a local college. One day a week of paid work, plus volunteering for an education charity, gave her just enough structure and stimulation. 'It's like I've got a foot in the door', she said, 'without stepping back onto the treadmill'. For Elaine, unretirement wasn't about money or obligation; it was about maintaining a sense of contribution.

PETER, 60: RECLAIMING RELEVANCE AND RHYTHM

Peter's story took a different shape. He had been nudged into early retirement during a company restructure. Though financially secure, he felt adrift within weeks. 'I lost my routine, my team, and my reason to get up in the morning.' Coaching helped him unpack what he truly missed: solving complex problems, collaborating with others, and feeling useful. Eventually, Peter took a short-term contract with a local design firm and now consults a few days a month. At first, he worried about how others would perceive his return to work – would it look like failure? But reframing helped him see it for what it was: a smart, self-directed reinvention that aligned with both his values and his energy.

MONIQUE, 70: RETURNING FOR CONNECTION

Then there's Monique whose unretirement wasn't about work at all; it was about people. After losing her partner and relocating to be near her daughter, she found herself lonely despite being 'happily retired' for years. Through coaching, she came to see that what she missed wasn't a job, but daily human interaction. She began working a couple of shifts a week at a local bookshop, a place filled with conversation and kindred spirits. 'It gives me a reason to put on lipstick', she said, 'and talk to people who love books'. Her work is light, joyful, and completely on her terms, and it brings her the connection she craved.

NAOMI, 56: A PAUSE, NOT A STOP

Naomi had left her role in marketing at 54, thinking she was ready to retire early. 'I thought I was done, the industry had changed so much, and I was tired', she said. But after a year of travel and rest, she noticed a new kind of restlessness creeping in. 'It wasn't about money. I just missed using my brain.'

Through coaching, Naomi reframed her early exit not as a retirement, but as a sabbatical. She began exploring part-time strategic roles and eventually joined a start-up as a fractional CMO, working two days a week. 'I still get to mentor, solve problems, and stay connected', she said, 'but now it's on my terms'.

Unretirement: A conscious return

Unretirement is not a failure to retire well; it's a reflection of evolving needs, energy, and desire. Some clients return for connection, others for structure or a renewed sense of usefulness. Coaching helps them assess readiness, clarify intention, and shape a return on their own terms. It's not going backward; it's moving forward with clarity and choice.

COACHING TOOL 9.2: Rethinking retirement, what's next for me?

A reflective guide for exploring unretirement and life redesign

This tool supports clients who are reconsidering full retirement, whether they're exploring a return to work, reshaping their daily rhythm, or redefining purpose in this next chapter. Use it for journalling, reflective dialogue, or in-session coaching.

Looking back

- What did you most enjoy about working life before you retired?
- What led you to step away from work, and was that choice fully yours?
- How did you imagine retirement would feel? How does the reality compare?

Exploring the pull

- What, if anything, do you find yourself missing?
- Is there a desire for more routine, stimulation, contribution, or social contact?
- What's motivating your interest in returning: income, identity, structure, purpose?

Designing your return

- If you were to return to work, what kind of role or rhythm would suit your current energy and lifestyle?
- What are your clear 'must-haves' and 'no-go' areas for this next phase?
- What boundaries would help protect your time, health, or freedom?

Reframing the narrative

- What story are you telling yourself about unretirement?
- Can you view this as a conscious redesign, not a reversal?
- What strengths, wisdom, or flexibility do you now bring that you didn't have before?

Reflection:
Unretirement isn't about going backward. It's about moving forward, on your own terms, with clarity, choice, and a renewed sense of self.

Navigating the emotional terrain of reinvention

While portfolio careers, self-employment, encore careers, and unretirement offer flexibility and deeper alignment, they also bring emotional complexity. These aren't just logistical changes; they're psychological transitions that can stir both liberation and disorientation.

As coaches, we must hold space for both excitement and grief, momentum and hesitation. The emotional terrain of later-life reinvention is rarely linear.

Letting go of the old story
For many, full-time work wasn't just a job; it was a source of identity, connection, and daily structure. Letting go of a role or title can feel like losing a sense of self. Even when chosen, these transitions may come with unexpected loss: of status, rhythm, or belonging.

Coaching can gently help clients name what they're carrying. 'What part of that identity do you want to keep? What might you set down?' Reframing allows them to see this next phase not as a downgrade, but as a conscious redesign.

Embracing multiple selves
Later-life work often invites a more plural identity: consultant and artist, mentor and carer, volunteer and freelancer. For some, this is empowering. For others, it feels chaotic or hard to explain. Coaching can offer coherence by anchoring in values, not titles. Identity doesn't need to be tidy to be true.

Living with uncertainty
Leaving conventional work can shake stability: financial, emotional, and psychological. Uncertainty is uncomfortable, especially for those used to control. But it can also be expansive.

We can support clients by creating inner and outer anchors: reflective practice, rhythm, accountability, or community. Encouraging an experimental mindset: 'this is a pilot, not a verdict', can ease pressure and open possibility.

Cultivating self-trust
At the core of all these transitions lies a quiet question: Can I trust myself now? Clients may compare themselves to their younger selves or societal norms. Coaching helps them let go of those scripts and tune into their own pace, energy, and curiosity. Self-trust isn't loud; it's the steady voice that says: 'I can do this differently and still do it well.'

COACHING TOOL 9.3: Who am I becoming now?

Exploring identity, transition, and emerging purpose

This reflection tool invites clients to explore evolving identity as they move beyond long-held roles, whether after retirement, redundancy, or career reinvention. It helps them navigate both the friction and the freedom of designing a working life that reflects their energy, values, and deeper self.

Encourage clients to take this slowly. Reflection may take time to surface. The goal is not to rush answers but to stay open to what is still unfolding.

1. **Honouring what was**
   - What role or title have you recently let go of, or are in the process of releasing?
   - What did that role give you, in terms of identity, belonging, or confidence?
   - What are you grateful for about that chapter of your life?
   - And what are you ready to leave behind?

2. **Naming what's emerging**
   - What new roles, identities, or projects are beginning to take shape?
   - Are there words or labels that feel like they're starting to fit, even if they're still unfamiliar?
   - What's giving you energy or sparking your curiosity right now?
   - If you had to describe your evolving working identity in three words, what would they be?

3. **Holding the in-between**
   - What's uncertain or uncomfortable about this transition?
   - What helps you stay grounded when the future feels undefined?
   - How can you offer yourself more patience or permission in this unfolding?

4. **Looking ahead**
   - What kind of rhythm or routine would support your wellbeing and creativity now?
   - What do you want your working life to *feel* like, even before you define what it is?
   - If this phase of your life were a book, what would the chapter title be?

Practical tools and pathways

This final section offers practical tools and prompts to support clients in moving from vision to small, meaningful steps on their own terms.

After exploring motivations, identity, and emotional readiness, many clients reach the point where they ask: *'What now?'* They've reimagined what work could look like in later life, but turning ideas into action can feel daunting without some structure. This section offers coaching tools and gentle pathways to help clients design work lives that are sustainable, flexible, and authentic.

The aim here isn't rigid planning or productivity pressure. It's about building a personal toolkit that supports grounded momentum and space for experimentation.

COACHING TOOL 9.4: Exploratory exercise: Designing a portfolio map or weekly rhythm

Visualising life balance, energy flow, and meaningful structure

One of the most supportive strategies at this stage of life is helping clients see their time, not just in terms of work, but in terms of life as a whole. This tool invites clients to map out an ideal week or month, exploring where their energy flows and what rhythms feel most sustainable.

Step 1: Identify the key domains

Begin by inviting clients to reflect on the broad areas that currently shape their time or that they would like to prioritise. Examples include:

- Paid work or side income;
- Caregiving or family commitments;
- Personal projects or creative expression;
- Volunteering or community involvement;
- Learning or skill building;
- Social connection;
- Movement or physical activity;
- Rest, reflection, or solitude.

Ask:

- What gives you energy?
- What tends to drain you?

Step 2: Create the visual map

Clients can sketch their time map in one of two ways:

- A **structured layout** (e.g. morning/afternoon/evening across seven days).
- A **freeform or circular design** showing proportional time or priorities.

Encourage them to use:

- **Colour coding** or symbols to represent different domains.
- **Energy markers** to note high/low energy times.
- **Flexible blocks** to reflect spaciousness and boundaries.

Step 3: Reflect and adjust

Once the map is drawn, invite reflection:

- Where does the week feel nourishing, and where does it feel overloaded?
- Are there enough anchors for wellbeing and rest?
- What's one small shift that could help bring this rhythm more into alignment with your energy and values?

Note: This 'Portfolio Life Canvas' is not a rigid plan. It's a *living document,* an evolving reflection of what matters now. It can be revisited and reshaped as needs, energy, or life circumstances change.

A printable version of this exercise is available in the resources toolkit online. To access, scan the QR code or visit the web address at the start of this book.

Self-employment essentials: Without overwhelm

Many clients are intrigued by self-employment but feel intimidated by the practicalities. Their questions often reveal a mix of curiosity and avoidance: *Do I need to register? What about paying tax? How do I price things?* As coaches, we're not there to give legal or financial advice, but we can demystify the process by helping them ask the right questions and access supportive resources.

A simple checklist can go a long way. Do they need to register as a sole trader or set up a limited company? Are they tracking income and expenses? What do they understand about tax obligations in their country? Would light training in invoicing, pricing, or marketing help build confidence? And beyond logistics, what boundaries do they need to set to protect their time, energy, or home space?

Signposting to local enterprise hubs, small business support centres, or peer-led start-up communities can be especially valuable for later-life entrepreneurs who want guidance without the jargon or overwhelm.

Building a support ecosystem

One of the most overlooked, but vital, elements of later-life career design is connection. Portfolio living and self-employment can be isolating without the camaraderie of colleagues or the shared structure of a team. Many clients don't initially realise how much they miss casual feedback, shared effort, or simply being seen.

Encourage clients to think creatively about support. This might include joining a mastermind group, setting up peer check-ins with others navigating similar transitions, finding or becoming a mentor, or simply spending time in co-working spaces or community networks. Some may benefit from attending industry events or local meetups, not to 'network' in the traditional sense, but to feel part of something larger.

Coaching conversations can explore what kind of support the client truly needs. Is it accountability? Encouragement? Practical tips? Emotional validation? Helping them name this can reduce resistance to asking for help or finding the right kind of company along the way.

Pathways into opportunity

Finally, clients often assume that opportunities must be formally structured or 'launched' to be valid. In reality, much of the richest work in later life emerges informally, through word of mouth, gentle visibility, and showing up with presence and value.

Coaching can help clients consider how to test ideas without big commitments. Perhaps they offer a taster session, share their interest with a former colleague, or run a small pilot project. Often, simply reaching out to a past contact or revisiting a community they care about can open unexpected doors.

The key here is low-risk exploration. Rather than aiming for a polished offer, encourage clients to follow curiosity, experiment gently, and let visibility grow from contribution, not self-promotion.

Small steps, taken with clarity and intention, can lay the groundwork for a meaningful working life in later years, one shaped not by old models of success, but by rhythm, relevance, and personal truth.

COACHING TOOL 9.5: Moving from ideas to action

Bridging reflection and implementation in later-life work transitions

This tool supports clients in moving from insight to action, especially when designing a portfolio life, exploring self-employment, or navigating the blurred space between work and personal renewal. Use these prompts across multiple sessions to clarify direction, reduce overwhelm, and support grounded next steps.

Mapping the portfolio
- What does a week of work and life that feels good look like for you?
- What kinds of work give you energy, and which types drain you?
- Where do you need more spaciousness, and where would structure support you?

Setting up for self-employment
- What practical steps would make you feel more confident about starting?
- What do you need to learn, and what can be 'good enough' for now?
- Where might you be overcomplicating things, and how could you simplify them?

Creating support
- Who are your go-to people when you need encouragement or clarity?
- What kind of support structure would help you feel less alone?
- What would it feel like to be part of a group or community doing similar things?

Opening doors
- Who already knows and trusts your work, and have you reached out to them?
- What's a small, low-risk way you could test an idea or offer?
- What would be a gentle, meaningful first step towards the work–life blend you're imagining?

Closing reflections: Crafting work that fits

In midlife and beyond, career paths are rarely linear, and 'retirement' is no longer a fixed destination. Instead, we see an expanding mosaic of work identities: part-time contributor, purpose-led founder, creative freelancer, mentor, volunteer, or joyful un-retiree.

This chapter has explored how clients can move beyond outdated expectations and towards self-authored working lives, shaped by values, energy, and an evolving sense of meaning.

Whether they're designing a portfolio life, stepping into self-employment, choosing an encore career or returning to work after a pause, clients are navigating more than logistics. They are:

- letting go of former identities;
- grappling with freedom and uncertainty;
- learning to trust themselves in unfamiliar terrain.

As coaches, our role is to help them:

- dream with grounding, and plan with curiosity;
- reframe identity as flexible, evolving, and multidimensional;
- move from self-doubt to self-trust; and
- take small, purposeful steps towards work that fits: in rhythm, scope, and meaning.

These are not fallback options. They are conscious, creative choices, blueprints for a more spacious and fulfilling future of work.

Because in later life, career is less about climbing and more about crafting.

In a nutshell

- Later-life work isn't a winding down; it's a reimagining.
- Portfolio careers, self-employment, and unretirement offer freedom and purpose, but also invite identity shifts and emotional complexity.
- With support and self-trust, clients can craft working lives that reflect not just who they were, but who they're becoming.
- These aren't smaller versions of work; they're deeper ones.

Chapter 10
Coaching with integrity: Ethical and psychological grounding in later life

> **Summary**
>
> *This chapter explores the emotional and ethical dimensions of later-life career coaching. It considers how ageing influences identity, readiness, and need, and examines how coaches can meet this complexity with presence, care, and integrity. Through psychological insights, ethical case vignettes, and reflective practices, it offers guidance on staying grounded, setting boundaries, and working skilfully with layered, human transitions.*

Holding space with integrity and care

Working with clients in midlife and beyond requires more than tools and techniques; it calls for emotional presence, ethical awareness, and deep respect for the human experience. At this life stage, career transitions are rarely just professional. They are intimately woven with questions of identity, loss, freedom, relevance, and mortality.

Clients may arrive carrying complex histories or invisible burdens. While some seek fresh opportunities, others carry shame, grief, anxiety, or declining health. As coaches, we must meet these clients with empathy and integrity, knowing when to support, when to pause, and when to refer.

This chapter explores both the psychological terrain of later-life coaching and the ethical responsibilities that underpin safe, responsible practice. It also highlights how client needs may differ by decade or life stage, not as rigid categories, but as evolving patterns, and how we can adapt our coaching accordingly.

The psychological landscape of later-life clients

Each stage of later life brings new psychological themes. While everyone is unique, common patterns emerge that influence how clients experience work, identity, and change. Though this section groups clients by decade, these are not fixed developmental markers. A 70-year-old may be chasing a new professional chapter, while a 50-something may already be seeking rhythm and legacy. What matters is meeting each client where they are, not only in age but in emotional readiness.

Clients in their 50s: Confidence, relevance, and responsibility

This is often a time of intense pressure and competing roles. Many clients are juggling peak career demands, caring for ageing parents or young children, and carrying financial responsibilities that limit flexibility. They may fear being 'aged out' or replaced. Some experience imposter syndrome following redundancy or a career break, while others appear confident externally but privately report deep self-doubt.

As coaches, we're often supporting clients to rebuild confidence, reclaim agency, and test possibilities without needing to prove their worth. One client, Dave, 59, had three children under five from a third marriage, a vivid reminder that life circumstances don't always follow age-based assumptions.

Clients in their 60s: Identity, loss, and redefinition

Many clients in this decade face the loss of a long-standing professional identity. The question 'Who am I now?' surfaces frequently. Alongside shifting roles, clients may be navigating grief, health changes, downsizing, or changes in family dynamics. Retirement may offer freedom but also feelings of invisibility or disconnection.

This stage often brings a desire to contribute, not through ambition, but through legacy. Coaching can support gentle identity reconstruction, experimentation, and the integration of inner reflection with outer structure.

> **JULIA, 61: WAS IT REALLY MY CHOICE?**
>
> Julia took early retirement after her role was made redundant, though several younger colleagues stayed. She describes it as a relief and a rejection all at once. 'Everyone told me to enjoy the freedom', she said, 'but I'm not sure it was my decision.' Julia's sessions focused on reclaiming authorship over her next chapter, not just accepting what had happened, but gently naming it and exploring what she truly wanted now.

Clients in their 70s and beyond: Meaning, mortality, and belonging

Some clients remain deeply engaged, driven by purpose and curiosity. Others feel cast aside, unsure how to contribute, or worried about fading relevance. This is often a highly reflective time, when spiritual or existential questions emerge. Clients may express concerns about cognitive decline, their legacy, or feeling unseen.

What they often seek is not activity for its own sake, but meaningful connection through storytelling, mentoring, intergenerational exchange, or community involvement. Coaching can provide space for life review, meaning-making, and helping them feel useful, not just busy.

Later-life coaching is developmental work. The challenge is to move beyond assumptions and instead ask: *'What stage of life is this client truly in, and how can I honour it?'*

Ethical vignettes: Coaching at the edges

The following real-world case examples illustrate common psychological and ethical dilemmas in later-life coaching.

MARK, 54: WASHED UP?

Client context: Mark was recently made redundant from a senior finance role. He describes himself as 'washed up' and expresses frequent fear of becoming unemployable. After a session, he emailed to ask, 'Do you think anyone will hire me again?'

Ethical challenge: How do you remain empathetic while avoiding dependency and over-reassurance? Are you slipping into a mentoring or advisory role unintentionally?

Coaching consideration: How can you reflect back the client's own strengths by inviting exploration rather than instruction, supporting confidence without assuming responsibility for outcomes?

CARLA, 62: LOSING THE POINT

Client context: Carla retired after 30 years in healthcare and now feels adrift. She speaks of low mood, lack of motivation, and says, 'I just don't see the point anymore'. Her energy is flat, and she avoids follow-through. She lives alone with limited social contact.

Ethical challenge: You sense this may be more than a career issue. How can you explore the limits of coaching, and when referral to therapy might be appropriate, without pathologising her experience?

Coaching consideration: How can you support Carla in reconnecting with her identity and purpose, while being mindful of potential underlying mental health concerns?

STAN, 74: STILL CAPABLE?

Client context: Stan wants to return to part-time project management. But he struggles to recall names and dates, and he repeats himself. He dismisses it as 'senior moments', yet you observe increasing disorganisation and frustration. He wants help updating his CV.

Ethical challenge: How do you navigate signs of possible cognitive decline without breaching trust or making assumptions? What if you're concerned about his readiness for work, but he disagrees?

Coaching consideration: What is your responsibility regarding safety, truth-telling, and dignity, and when is it time to involve other professionals?

NAOMI, 59: EXPERT OR ENABLER?

Client context: Naomi is exploring self-employment after years in the charity sector. She asks about registering as a sole trader, managing tax, and building a website. You have experience in this area and begin offering tips, but notice she's treating them as instructions.

Ethical challenge: Where is the line between helpful context and slipping into consultancy or financial advice? Are you empowering Naomi to choose, or replacing her agency?

Coaching consideration: How can you provide useful guidance while remaining in a facilitative coaching role? What boundaries do you need to maintain to keep coaching client-led?

> ### Ethical coaching in later life: Boundaries with care
>
> **Career work in later life is deeply psychological.**
>
> Clients may bring grief, identity loss, confidence wounds, or existential questions. Listen well, but know your boundaries.
>
> **Stay in the coaching lane.**
>
> When clients seek reassurance, therapy, or financial/legal advice, pause. Reflect, redirect, or refer. Coaching is facilitative, not directive.
>
> **Compassion doesn't mean over-functioning.**
>
> Support without rescuing. Validate without fixing. Empathise without assuming responsibility.
>
> **Name what you see, gently.**
>
> If you're concerned about wellbeing, decline, or safety, raise it with care and clarity. Don't avoid difficult truths.
>
> **Supervision is essential.**
>
> Later-life transitions are emotionally layered. Bring dilemmas to supervision. You are not meant to carry this alone.
>
> *'Our job isn't to rescue or redirect. It's to walk beside people as they remember who they are and what they still have to offer.'*

Ethical boundaries and responsibilities

Ethical coaching with later-life clients goes beyond adhering to frameworks or avoiding wrongdoing. It means consistently returning to the core principles of informed consent, psychological safety, professional clarity, and human dignity, especially in work that touches on identity, loss, mortality, and emotional vulnerability.

This section offers a reflective lens on key ethical responsibilities across the coaching arc, from contracting and active listening to recognising red flags and ending well. Rather than a rigid checklist, consider this a practice guide to revisit throughout your work, especially with complex or emotionally layered clients.

Before coaching begins: Clarity and consent

Ethical practice starts before the first session. Clients in later life often arrive with high hopes and deep needs, so it's essential to clearly define the purpose and limits of the coaching relationship.

Have you explained the scope of your work; what coaching is (and isn't)? Have you discussed boundaries around confidentiality, data use, and what happens if either of you feels coaching is no longer the right fit?

It's also important to have a clear referral policy: When and how will you signpost clients to a therapist, medical professional, or financial/legal expert if needed? Laying this foundation early on sets the tone for safety, respect, and autonomy.

During coaching: Presence and role clarity

Coaching later-life clients requires sensitivity to what is spoken and what is not. As you listen, are you attuned to what lies beneath the surface? Are you noticing emotional themes such as shame, grief, or fear of irrelevance? Sometimes, the client may not name these directly, but they're present in energy, tone, or hesitancy.

It's vital to hold a facilitative stance. Are you supporting inquiry, or sliding into advice-giving? Do you find yourself offering solutions where reflection would serve better?

Stay alert to signs of dependency or idealisation. If a client continually seeks reassurance, avoids closure, or appears emotionally flat, it may be time to slow down and check in. A simple reflection like *'How are you finding these sessions?'* can create space for honest feedback.

When things get blurry: Recognising red flags

Supervision becomes essential when coaching begins to drift beyond its boundaries. Notice if:

- Sessions start feeling more like therapy than coaching.
- You or the client carry a strong emotional charge after sessions.
- Clients share material that feels outside your scope, such as suicidal thoughts, intense loneliness, or unresolved trauma.
- The conversation begins to edge into advice around finances, health, or legal decisions.

These moments aren't failures. They're signals, invitations to pause, reflect, and seek supervision or peer support. Naming what you notice can prevent harm and support ethical alignment.

Beyond the session: Your inner landscape

Ethical practice includes noticing your own reactions. Do you find yourself overly invested in a client's outcome? Do you avoid certain topics, or feel responsible for how the client feels? Are there particular stories or emotions that stay with you after a session?

These are signs to take into supervision. Reflective practice is especially important in later-life work, where your own ageing assumptions or emotional responses might quietly shape the space.

Ask yourself:

- What's mine and what's theirs?
- Where might I be over-functioning?
- Am I holding space neutrally, or slipping into fixing, advising, or projecting?

Holding boundaries isn't about emotional distance; it's about ethical closeness with clarity.

Ending well: Closure as an ethical act

Closure is part of the coaching process, not an afterthought. Clients in later life may have ambivalent endings, especially if work has felt supportive or rare in its quality of attention. Ethical endings include preparing for transition, reflecting on progress, and co-creating a meaningful sense of closure.

Ask:

- Have we named what's been achieved, what's emerging, and what remains uncertain?
- Have I offered appropriate signposting if further support is needed?
- Does the ending feel clean and kind, or rushed and ambiguous?

Ongoing practice: A living ethical compass

Use these reflections regularly, especially with clients navigating non-linear paths, health challenges, or existential shifts. Ethical work in later-life coaching is rarely black and white; it asks us to stay curious, reflective, and humble.

Ethics aren't just about rules; they're about relationship, responsibility, and the courage to hold complexity with care.

Reflective practice and supervision in later-life career coaching

Ethical awareness in coaching isn't only about what we *say*; it's also about what we *feel*. It lives in the pauses between questions, in the inner stirrings that arise when a client's story echoes our own. That's where reflective practice and supervision matter most, not just as professional responsibilities, but as lifelines.

Throughout this book, you've already encountered reflective prompts woven into earlier chapters, moments to stop, notice, and inquire. This section builds on that foundation, deepening the invitation to cultivate reflection as an ongoing, sustaining discipline in your coaching life.

Working with clients in midlife and beyond can be some of the most meaningful work we do, and also the most emotionally layered. These conversations are often about more than careers. They touch on grief, reinvention, ageing, identity, and belonging. This is life work, not just job work. And it asks something of us, too.

Chapter 10: Coaching with Integrity: Ethical and Psychological Grounding in Later Life

As coaches, we may find ourselves touched by what clients bring: a partner's death, a forced retirement, a longing for relevance, a fear of decline. These moments can stir something personal, reflections on our own identity, purpose, or mortality. Reflective practice and supervision help us meet these echoes with steadiness. They return us to presence, perspective, and integrity.

Reflective practice: Deepening awareness

Reflective practice is the ongoing discipline of pausing to notice what's happening in the client, in ourselves, and in the space between. It isn't about self-critique; it's about alignment. It's a return to our values, our role, and our human limitations.

You might ask yourself:

- What am I noticing in this session: emotionally, energetically, relationally?
- What assumptions or responses am I bringing in, and where do they come from?
- What stayed with me after this session, and why?

Some coaches journal, others use voice notes, supervision logs, or peer dialogue. It's not the format that matters. It's the regular act of noticing, so the work gets metabolised, rather than carried unconsciously.

Supervision: Lifeline and mirror

Supervision is not just a place for technical support. It's a relational practice, a mirror for our development, a container for emotional residue, and a space to bring ethical uncertainty without shame. In later-life career coaching, supervision often invites questions that reach beyond method:

- Am I over-identifying with this client, or protecting myself by disconnecting?
- Is the sadness I feel mine, or theirs?
- Am I coaching, or slipping into therapist, rescuer, or expert?

These tensions are natural. Clients may remind us of our parents, our former selves, or our future. Good supervision allows us to explore those reactions with curiosity, not judgement, and to return to our practice steadier and clearer.

It also sharpens our ethical lens: Are we holding ethical clarity? Are we honouring autonomy while still offering structure? Regular supervision strengthens the work and protects the relationship.

Reflective prompts for coaches

These questions can be used in journaling, group reflection, or supervision. They help you stay centred, responsive, and honest in your work:

- What part of this client's story am I still carrying, and what does that tell me?
- Where do I feel most grounded in my coaching right now, and where am I out of my depth?
- What thoughts or feelings does this client stir in me around ageing, loss, or purpose?
- When do I find myself slipping into advice, reassurance, or rescue, and how can I return to presence?
- These aren't just prompts for difficult sessions; they're companions for deep work.

> **Reflection tool: Navigating ethical edges**
>
> Use these guiding questions to deepen your awareness of emotional activation, role clarity, and boundary sensitivity in your coaching:
>
> - Where do I feel most emotionally activated in my coaching work?
> - What boundaries feel easiest to hold, and which feel porous?
> - When do I feel most helpful, and is that always ethical?
> - What part of this is about my own need to rescue, fix, or be needed?
>
> These are not just signs of struggle; they're invitations to deepen your ethical grounding.

A profession that keeps evolving

Career coaching with later-life clients invites us to evolve alongside them. As they reflect on their legacy, we're invited to reflect on ours. As they face uncertainty, we're called to meet it with courage and clarity.

The most effective coaches bring more than strategy. They bring presence. They hold space not just for motivation, but for mystery. They coach with humility and remain open to learning, questioning, and growing.

When done well, this work becomes more than support; it becomes a shared inquiry into what it means to live fully, age honestly, and change with dignity.

Final reflections: The ethical invitation

Ethical coaching in later life is not just about staying within scope; it's about meeting clients with humility, presence, and care. Through reflection, supervision, and honest self-awareness, we stay responsive to the complexity of later-life work and bring the thoughtfulness this stage of life deserves. In doing so, we keep the coaching space grounded, ethical, and truly human.

This work, like ageing itself, is never static. It keeps unfolding. In my own journey, this book is one part of a broader inquiry. As I continue to explore how people live, work, and grow in later life, I'll be deepening these themes further in *Olderhood Unfolding* – a book for those navigating this stage firsthand.

Because in truth, the work we do as coaches doesn't just support others. It invites us, too, into a more honest, humane, and wholehearted way of growing older. And perhaps that's the true legacy of this work – that in supporting others, we learn to grow with greater grace ourselves.

In a nutshell

- Ethical coaching in later life isn't about having all the answers. It's about staying present, curious, and clear.
- Coaches must know when to support, when to reflect, and when to refer, always in service of the client's safety and growth.
- Supervision, deep listening, and ethical clarity help us navigate complexity with integrity and honour the lives entrusted to us.

Chapter 11
Coaching at the edge of change: Supporting what comes after work

> **Summary**
>
> *This final chapter reflects on the evolving nature of later-life career coaching, exploring how identity, work, and ageing are shifting in a changing world. It highlights emerging trends, systemic challenges, and the role of reflective, human-centred practice in supporting this transition, both for clients and coaches.*

Looking back

Throughout this book, we've explored the increasingly complex, nuanced, and deeply human terrain of midlife and later-life career development. No longer a linear path marked by steady progression and an abrupt end at retirement, the modern career journey for those aged 50 and beyond is being reshaped by longevity, changing workplace expectations, shifting values, and evolving personal circumstances.

We've seen how career coaching in this space requires a broader lens, one that goes beyond employability and CVs. It calls for a deeper understanding of identity, purpose, autonomy, loss, and reinvention. Midlife transitions are often about more than just work; they can involve caregiving, health shifts, bereavement, or a reappraisal of what truly matters. These are not simply logistical hurdles to overcome but life transitions that need space, compassion, and skilled coaching support.

We've also highlighted the diversity of client needs. Some seek re-entry into the workplace, others want to downshift, explore portfolio careers, or move into self-employment. Some face redundancy or marginalisation, while others feel ready to step into something new but undefined. The common thread is change, sometimes chosen, sometimes imposed, and the need for guidance that is age-aware, person-centred, and psychologically informed.

Across the chapters, I've provided tools, frameworks, and reflective practices that support coaches in navigating this work with integrity. From identity shifts and skill translation to phased retirement and unretirement, career coaching in midlife and beyond is as much about listening and reframing as it is about action planning.

Ultimately, this is work that affirms the continuing value of experience, the possibility of growth at every stage, and the human desire for meaning, even, and perhaps especially, in later life.

Future landscape

The world of work is undergoing rapid transformation and so too are the lives of those in midlife and beyond. With populations ageing and longevity increasing, traditional notions of retirement are being dismantled. Many people will live a third of their adult lives 'post-retirement'. This extended phase of life brings opportunity, but also uncertainty.

Flexible work, hybrid models, and digital platforms are creating new possibilities for contribution across the lifespan. People are working longer, but differently, with more emphasis on autonomy, purpose, and balance. We are seeing the rise of phased retirements, portfolio careers, encore work, and 'unretirement' not out of necessity alone, but from a desire to remain engaged and useful.

At the same time, systemic challenges remain. Ageism, lack of employer flexibility, health inequalities, and digital exclusion continue to shape the experience of older workers. These realities call for both advocacy and innovation.

For career coaches, this means adapting to a landscape that is less predictable, more fluid, and increasingly age-diverse. Supporting clients through this requires both practical tools and a broader developmental perspective, one that honours the individual's evolving sense of self in the context of a changing world.

Chapter 11: Coaching at the Edge of Change: Supporting What Comes After Work

Reflection tool: Future-sensing as a coach

Use these prompts to anticipate how you might evolve alongside your clients:

- How is my own career model evolving as I age?
- What societal shifts am I noticing, and how do they impact the people I work with?
- Where might I need to expand my knowledge or collaborations to remain relevant?

Evolving role of the coach

As the context changes, so too does the role of the coach. Career professionals working with midlife and later-life clients are increasingly becoming guides through transition, not only helping clients find work, but also supporting them to redefine identity, navigate uncertainty, and align their lives with personal values.

This work straddles career and life, strategy and meaning. It requires us to be skilled in reframing narratives, holding space for ambiguity, and helping clients integrate the many threads of their lives, not just their work history. The traditional tools of career coaching still matter, but they must sit alongside a broader, more psychologically aware approach.

Coaches must also be attuned to grief, loss, reinvention, and resistance. Clients may be grappling with letting go of a career that once defined them, managing long-term health conditions, or responding to caregiving responsibilities. Others are energised, curious, and ready for something new, but unsure how to move forward.

In this landscape, the career coach becomes a steady companion: reflective, informed, and committed to the client's autonomy. There is also a growing need for collaboration with other professionals, including financial advisers, therapists, GPs, and HR specialists to offer truly holistic support.

> **WLADISLAV, 57: 'WHAT NOW?'**
>
> Wladislav had worked at three different media companies by the time he was 50. Layoffs were routine, and each reinvention felt harder. Eventually, he pivoted to content strategy for a tech firm but felt like a dinosaur in meetings. 'They talked in memes and Slack emojis', he said. 'I still write full sentences.' The turning point came when he admitted: 'Maybe I've outgrown the chase.'
>
> Through coaching, Wladislav explored what he wanted next; not another brand or platform, but something slower, more human. He began training part-time in psychotherapy, drawing on his lifelong fascination with stories and the inner life. 'I used to write profiles of rock stars', he said. 'Now I sit with people and hear what's real.' His income is lower. His sense of meaning is deeper.
>
> **Coaching reflection:** When clients feel they've outgrown the pace or values of their former industry, coaching can help them pivot towards work that feels more human, grounded, and aligned with who they're becoming.

Technology and AI

Technology is reshaping how we work and how we coach. From job search platforms and AI-driven CV tools to online learning and virtual coaching environments, digital innovation can enhance the coaching process, offering convenience, personalisation, and access.

Yet as automation increases, so does the value of human connection. For many clients, particularly those navigating identity change or loss, the relational aspect of coaching – being seen, heard, and valued – is irreplaceable.

As coaches, we need to be digitally competent and ethically thoughtful. Questions about algorithmic bias, privacy, data use, and accessibility are becoming more pressing. At the same time, we can embrace digital tools that extend our reach, such as group coaching platforms, asynchronous tools, or hybrid models of delivery.

Technology will continue to evolve. Our task is to stay grounded in human-centred practice, using digital tools to support, not replace, the reflective depth that is the hallmark of effective coaching. As AI continues to advance, coaches must also reflect on how emerging tools may replicate or challenge human biases, and how to maintain ethics in an automated world.

Life review and meaning

As clients move beyond full-time work, whether through retirement, reinvention, or a blend of both, their questions often shift. They move from 'What's next?' to 'What matters?' These are not just career questions; they are life questions.

As coaches, our role often becomes less about offering direction and more about allowing room for reflection, integration, and meaning-making.

If this work resonates with you and the clients you serve, my next book, *Olderhood Unfolding*, is written with you in mind. It offers tools, stories, and guided practices, including this one, to support deeper conversations in later life.

Reflective practice: Life review and meaning (from olderhood unfolding)

Reflections on a life well lived

Use these prompts to support deeper inquiry with clients, or as part of your own reflective practice:

- What truly matters now?
- What brings joy, meaning, or peace?
- How do you make sense of the life you've lived so far?

These questions invite pause, not just to plan what's next, but to reflect on what's essential. This is where coaching becomes not only practical, but transformational.

Developing the coach's reflective practice

This work calls for continual reflection, not only on our coaching practice but on ourselves as practitioners. Working with ageing clients often stirs personal questions about our own later lives, our values, and our relationship to change, uncertainty, and legacy.

Supervision and continuing professional development are essential. Just as essential is the willingness to examine our own assumptions about age, success, decline, and productivity. We carry the cultural narratives we've inherited, and we need to stay alert to how these shape our coaching presence, language, and expectations.

> **Reflective practice: Coach reflection on ageing and self**
>
> - How do I personally relate to ageing and later life?
> - What unconscious biases might I hold about work, retirement, or productivity?
> - Where do I feel most challenged in this work, and what does that tell me?
> - What gives me energy in this work? What drains it?
> - Are you modelling a positive, open mindset about ageing in your own life and work?
>
> By staying reflective and open, we deepen our presence, sharpen our insight, and ensure that our coaching remains responsive to the evolving needs of those we serve.
>
> As we look ahead, it's just as important to return to the heart of this work, to the intention behind it, and to the quiet integrity of showing up with care.

Closing reflections

Career coaching for midlife and beyond is not simply about helping people find jobs. It is about affirming possibility, dignity, and meaning in a phase of life that is too often overlooked or misunderstood.

As coaches, we are invited to accompany people through moments of doubt, reinvention, and awakening, helping them uncover new ways to grow, contribute, and connect. In doing so, we're not just supporting individuals; we're helping to reshape how society understands ageing.

This is slow, sometimes messy work. But it matters. And it will only become more important in the years ahead.

Let us meet this moment with wisdom, humility, and imagination, and support those with whom we work to do the same.

May we continue to walk beside those navigating later life with courage, clarity, and the quiet confidence that change is always possible.

Rather than managing ageing as a problem, this work encourages us to engage with it as an evolving experience, rich with insight, purpose, and the potential for continued growth.

Chapter 11: Coaching at the Edge of Change: Supporting What Comes After Work

In a nutshell

- Midlife and later-life coaching is no longer niche; it's vital.
- As people live and work longer, the need for age-aware, human-centred career support is growing.
- Coaches must be reflective, adaptable, and willing to meet both practical needs and deeper questions about identity, purpose, and contribution.

Looking ahead: Deeper reflections on life after work

As this book closes, many readers, whether coaches or individuals in transition, may find themselves asking not just 'what's next in my career?' but 'what's next in my life?'

We move from what we do to who we are now.

From structured goals to deeper inquiry.

From navigating work to navigating life.

For those entering a stage beyond full-time employment, whether retirement, reinvention, or something in between, new questions emerge:

- What truly matters now?
- What brings me joy, meaning, or peace?
- How do I make sense of the life I've lived so far?

My future work continues this journey, offering reflections and tools for navigating later life with depth, vitality, and renewed purpose.

Forthcoming work:

- *ThriveSpan: A New Map for Meaningful Later Life:* introducing a practical model for wellbeing, purpose, and fulfilment beyond full-time work (1 March, 2026).
- *Olderhood Unfolding* (planned for later in 2026): a reflective exploration of ageing as a personal and existential journey.

Further resources

For professionals:

Alongside my writing, I value engaging with coaches and practitioners who are supporting clients through later-life transitions.

My focus is on creating thoughtful spaces for dialogue and reflection – through guest sessions, workshops, and small groups. These invite us to move beyond standard over-50s retirement coaching and into more expansive conversations about ageing and olderhood.

To stay updated, visit www.denisetaylor.co.uk or connect with me on LinkedIn.

Further reading and sources by chapter

This list offers suggested reading for those who wish to explore the ideas in each chapter more deeply. It includes foundational theories, contemporary research, and practical resources relevant to midlife and later-life career development.

Chapter 1: Why midlife and retirement coaching matters

- Erikson, E. H. (1982). *The Life Cycle Completed.* New York: Norton. *(Outlines the psychosocial stages of human development, including later-life integration.)*
- Jung, C. G. (1933). *Modern Man in Search of a Soul.* London: Routledge. *(Introduces Jung's ideas on individuation and the inner life in adulthood.)*
- Rauch, J. (2019). *The Happiness Curve: Why Life Gets Better After Midlife.* London: Green Tree.
- Taylor, D. (2022). *Rethinking Retirement for Positive Ageing.* London: Routledge. *(Drawn from the author's PhD research on meaning in later life.)*

Chapter 2: Understanding midlife career transitions

- https://www.brucefeiler.com/books-articles/life-is-in-the-transitions/ (Life Quakes) 2021.
- Hudson, F. M. (1999). *The Adult Years: Mastering the Art of Self-Renewal.* San Francisco: Jossey-Bass. *(Explores adult development and the cycles of self-renewal across the lifespan.)*
- Rotter, J. B. (1966). Generalized expectancies for internal versus external control of reinforcement. *Psychological Monographs: General and Applied, 80*(1), 1–28.

Chapter 3: Coaching for career reinvention in midlife

- https://www.thephoenixgroup.com/our-impact/people/living-longer/changing-careers-can-help-you-shape-the-future-you-want/ *(Discusses midlife career reinvention and narratives of personal change.)*
- McKinsey Health Institute. (2024). *The New Map of Life: A Conversation with Andrew J. Scott.* (Interview exploring 'evergreening' strategies: health, learning, purpose, and social capital.)

- Office for National Statistics. (2023). *Past and Projected Period and Cohort Life Expectancy Tables.* https://www.ons.gov.uk *(Official UK data projecting longevity trends into the 21st century.)*
- Scott, A. (2024). *The Evergreening Economy: Rethinking Age, Work, and Vitality in Longer Lives.* (Key ideas from Andrew Scott's work on longevity strategy and thriving across extended lifespans.)

Chapter 4: The psychology of retirement and identity shifts

- https://agewave.com/what-we-do/landmark-research-and-consulting/research-studies/work-and-retirement-myths-and-motivations/
- https://psyche.co/guides/how-to-find-meaning-in-your-life-as-a-buffer-against-anxiety *(Meaning in life audit)*
- https://theconversation.com/retirement-doesnt-just-raise-financial-concerns-it-can-also-mean-feeling-unmoored-and-irrelevant-233963
- Joshi, P., et al. (2023). *Social connections as determinants of cognitive health and dementia: A scoping review of meta-analyses and systematic reviews. Frontiers in Aging Neuroscience, 15,* Article 11058077. https://doi.org/10.3389/fnagi.2023.11058077 (PMC)
- Jung, C. G. (1933). *Modern Man in Search of a Soul.* See Chapter 1.
- Levy, B. (2022). *Breaking the Age Code: How Your Beliefs About Aging Determine How Long and Well You Live.* London: Penguin Random House.
- Levy, B. R., Slade, M. D., Kunkel, S. R., & Kasl, S. V. (2002). Longevity increased by positive self-perceptions of aging. *Journal of Personality and Social Psychology, 83*(2), 261–270.
- McAdams, D. P., & de St. Aubin, E. (1992). A theory of generativity and its assessment through self-report, behavioral acts, and narrative themes in autobiography. *Journal of Personality and Social Psychology, 62*(6), 1003–1015. *(Builds on Erikson's work with a deeper look at how generativity plays out in adult lives and identity.)* https://doi.org/10.1037/0022-3514.62.6.1003
- Meng, A., et al. (2017). The impact of retirement on age-related cognitive decline: A systematic review. *BMC Geriatrics, 17,* 156. https://doi.org/10.1186/s12877-017-0556-7 (BioMed Central)
- Pillemer, K. (2020). *The Gift of Experience: Wisdom for Meaningful Aging.* New York: Avery. *(Explores how generativity, legacy, and life review contribute to later-life purpose and connection.)*
- Taylor, D. (2022). *Rethinking Retirement for Positive Ageing.* London: Routledge.

- Waldinger, R., & Schulz, M. (2023). *The Good Life: Lessons from the World's Longest Scientific Study of Happiness*. London: Penguin Books.
- Xue, B., et al. (2018). Effect of retirement on cognitive function: the Whitehall II cohort study. *Memory & Cognition*, *46*(5), 751–761.

Chapter 5: Designing a meaningful life after full-time work

- Pfund, G. N., Lewis, N. A., & Hill, P. L. (2024). Sense of purpose and cognitive functioning: A 10-year longitudinal study of older adults. *Psychological Science*, *35*(1), 23–33. https://doi.org/10.1177/09567976231217758

Chapter 6: Practical tools for career coaches

- Schön, D. A. (1983). *The Reflective Practitioner*. New York: Basic Books.
- Stober, D. R., & Grant, A. M. (Eds.). (2006). *Evidence Based Coaching Handbook: Putting Best Practices to Work for Your Clients*. Hoboken, NJ: John Wiley & Sons, Inc.

Chapter 8: Navigating ageism and changing workplace dynamics

- For further evidence on employer attitudes and structural barriers, see the CIPD's 2022 report, Understanding Older Workers. – https://www.cipd.org/uk/knowledge/reports/understanding-older-workers/
- Rock, D. (2006). *Quiet Leadership: Six Steps to Transforming Performance at Work*. New York: HarperBusiness.

Chapter 9: Portfolio careers, self-employment, encore careers, and unretirement

- https://encore.org/marc-freedman-bios/ Highlights work on purpose and social impact in later-life careers.

Chapter 11: Coaching at the edge of change: Supporting what comes after work

- Hillman, J. (1999). *The Force of Character and the Lasting Life*. New York: Ballantine Books.
- Tornstam, L. (2005). *Gerotranscendence: A Developmental Theory of Positive Aging*. New York: Springer Publishing Company.

DISCOVER TROTMAN'S
CAREER DEVELOPMENT INSTITUTE
COLLECTION

The Career Professional's Guide to Research
9781911724599
By Emma Bolger

Equity, Diversity, and Inclusion in Career Development
9781911724698
By Ifza Shakoor

The Career Development Professional's AI Toolkit
9781911724650
By Michael Larbalestier and Marianne Wilson

Sustainable Careers
9781911724537
By Liz Painter

Career Coaching for Midlife and Beyond
9781911724711
By Denise Taylor

The Career Development Professional's Survival Guide
9781911724674
By Jules Benton and Chris Targett

Enhance your careers library with careers essentials, free resources and expert articles

Visit www.trotman.co.uk